Free Stuff for Kids

Our Pledge

We have collected and examined the best free and up-to-a-dollar offers we could find. Each supplier in this book has promised to honor properly made requests for **single items** through **2001**. Though mistakes do happen, we are doing our best to make sure this book really works.

—*The Free Stuff Editors*

Meadowbrook Press
Distributed by Simon & Schuster
New York

The Free Stuff Editors

Publisher: Bruce Lansky
Coordinating Editor: Megan McGinnis
Administrative Assistant: Beth Madsen
Copywriter: Megan McGinnis
Copy Editor: Christine Zuchora-Walske
Production Manager: Paul Woods
Desktop Publishing: Danielle White

ISBN: 0-88166-372-7
Simon & Schuster Ordering # 0-689-84078-0

ISSN: 1056-9693
24th Edition

Published by Meadowbrook Press, 5451 Smetana Drive, Minnetonka, MN 55343

www.meadowbrookpress.com

BOOK TRADE DISTRIBUTION by Simon & Schuster, a division of Simon and Schuster, Inc., 1230 Avenue of the Americas, New York, NY 10020

04 03 02 01 00   5 4 3 2 1

Printed in the United States of America

Contents

Thank You

To Pat Blakely, Barbara Haislet, and Judith Hentges for creating and publishing the original *Rainbow Book*, proving that kids, parents, and teachers would respond enthusiastically to a source of free things by mail. They taught us the importance of carefully checking the quality of each item and doing our best to make sure that each and every request is satisfied.

Our heartfelt appreciation goes to hundreds of organizations and individuals for making this book possible. They and the editors of this book have a common goal: to make it possible for kids to reach out and discover the world by themselves.

Read This First

About This Book

Free Stuff for Kids lists hundreds of items you can send away for. The Free Stuff Editors have examined every item and think each is among the best offers available. There are no trick offers—only safe, fun, and informative things you'll like!

This book is designed for kids who can read and write. The directions on the following pages explain exactly how to request an item. Read the instructions carefully so you know how to send a request. Making sure you've filled out a request correctly is easy—just complete the *Free Stuff for Kids* **Checklist** on page 8. Half the fun is using the book on your own. The other half is getting a real reward for your efforts!

Each year the Free Stuff Editors create a new edition of this book by taking out old items, inserting new ones, and updating addresses and prices. It is important for you to use an updated edition because the suppliers only honor properly made requests for single items for the **current** edition. If you use this edition after **2001**, your request will not be honored.

Reading Carefully

Read the descriptions of the offers carefully to find out exactly what you're getting. Here are a couple of tips:

- A pamphlet is usually one sheet of paper folded over and printed on both sides.
- A booklet is usually larger than a pamphlet and contains more pages, but it's smaller than a book.

Following Directions

It's important to follow each supplier's directions. On one offer, you might need to use a postcard. On another offer, you might be asked to include money or a long self-addressed stamped envelope. If you do not follow the directions **exactly**, you might not get your request. Unless the directions tell you differently, ask for only **one** of anything you send for. Family members or classmates using the same book must send **separate** requests.

Sending Postcards

A postcard is a small card you can write on and send through the mail without an envelope. Many suppliers offering free items require you to send requests on postcards. Please do this. It saves them the time it takes to open many envelopes.

The post office sells postcards with preprinted postage. You can also buy postcards at a drugstore and put special postcard stamps on them yourself. Your local post office can tell you how much a postcard stamp currently costs. Postcards with pictures on them are usually more expensive. You must use a postcard that is at least 3½ by 5½ inches. Your postcards should be addressed like the one below:

Your Name
Your Address
City, State Zip Code

Supplier's Name
Supplier's Address
City, State Zip Code

Front

Dear Sir or Madam:

Please send me some super cool stuff. Thank you very much.

Sincerely,
Your Name
Your Address
City, State Zip Code

Back

- Use a ballpoint pen. Pencil can be difficult to read, and felt-tip pens often smear.
- **Neatly print** the supplier's address in the center of the side of the postcard that has the postage. Put your return address in the upper left corner of that side, too.
- **Neatly print** your request, your name, and your address on the blank side of the postcard.
- Do not abbreviate the name of your street or city.

Sending Letters

Your letters should look like the one below:

- Use a ballpoint pen. Pencil can be difficult to read, and felt-tip pens often smear.
- **Neatly print** the name of the item you want exactly as you see it in the directions.
- **Neatly print** your own name and address at the bottom of the letter. (Do not abbreviate the name of your street or city.)
- If you're including coins, first-class stamps, or a long self-addressed stamped envelope, say so in the letter. And be sure to enclose the coins, the stamps, or the envelope!
- Put a **first-class stamp** on any envelope you send to suppliers in the United States. Envelopes you send to suppliers in Canada will need extra postage. You can find out how much postage to Canada costs at your local post office. You can also get stamps at the post office.
- **Neatly print** the supplier's address in the center of the envelope and your return address in the upper left corner.
- If you're sending many letters at once, make sure you put each letter in the correct envelope.

Sending a Long Self-Addressed Stamped Envelope

If the directions say to enclose a long self-addressed stamped envelope, here's how to do it:

• Use a ballpoint pen. Pencil can be hard to read, and felt-tip pens often smear.

• **Neatly print** your name and address in the center of a **10-inch-long envelope** as if you were mailing it to yourself. Print your return address in the upper left corner of the envelope, too. Put a **first-class stamp** on it, or put more than one first-class stamp on it if the directions say so.

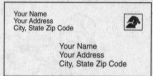

Your Name
Your Address
City, State Zip Code

Your Name
Your Address
City, State Zip Code

• **Fold up** (but don't seal!) the long self-addressed stamped envelope and put it inside another **10-inch-long envelope** along with your letter to the supplier. Put a **first-class stamp** on the second envelope, too.

• **Neatly print** the supplier's address in the center of the outside envelope and your return address in the upper left corner.

Sending Money

Many of the suppliers in this book are not charging you for their items. However, the cost of postage and handling is high today, and suppliers must charge you for this. If the directions say to enclose money, **you must do so**. Here are a few rules about sending money:

• Tape the coins to your letter or an index card so they won't break out of the envelope.

• Don't stack your coins in the envelope.

• Don't use pennies or nickels. These coins will add weight to your envelope, and you may need to use more than one stamp.

• If an item costs $1.00, send a one-dollar bill instead of coins. Don't tape dollar bills.

• Send U.S. money only.

• If a grownup is helping you, he or she may write a check **unless the directions tell you not to send checks**.

• Send all money directly to the suppliers; their addresses are listed with their offers.

Getting Your Stuff

Expect to wait four to eight weeks for your stuff to arrive. Sometimes you have to wait longer. Remember, suppliers get thousands of requests each year. Please be patient! If you wait a long time and your offer still doesn't come, you may be using an old book. This is the **2001** edition; the offers in this book will be good only for **2000** and **2001**!

Making Sure You Get Your Request

The Free Stuff Editors have tried to make the directions for using this book as clear as possible to make sure you get what you send for. But you must follow **all** of the directions **exactly** as they're written, or the supplier **will not be able to answer your request**. If you're confused about the directions, ask a grownup to help you.

Dos and Don'ts

- **Do** use a ballpoint pen. Typing and using a computer are okay, too.
- **Do** print. Cursive writing can be difficult to read.
- **Do** print your name, address, and Zip Code clearly and fully on the postcard or on the envelope **and** on the letter you send—sometimes envelopes and letters get separated after they reach the supplier.
- **Do** send the correct amount of U.S. money, but don't use pennies or nickels.
- **Do** tape the coins to your letter or to an index card. If you don't tape them, the coins might rip the envelope and fall out.
- **Do** use a **10-inch-long** self-addressed stamped envelope when the instructions ask for a long envelope.

- **Do not** use this **2001** edition **after** 2001.
- **Do not** ask for more than **one** of an item, unless the directions say you can.
- **Do not** stack coins in the envelope.
- **Do not** seal your long self-addressed stamped envelope. The suppliers need to be able to put the item you ordered in the envelope you send.
- **Do not** ask Meadowbrook Press to send you any of the items listed in the book unless you are ordering the Meadowbrook offers on pages 65 and 70–71. Meadowbrook Press does not carry items belonging to other suppliers. It does not supply refunds either.

Follow all the instructions to avoid disappointment!

What to Do If You Aren't Satisfied

If you have complaints about any offer, or if you don't receive the items you sent for within eight to ten weeks, contact the Free Stuff Editors. If you have a complaint about an Internet offer, please see page 99. Before you complain, please reread the directions. Are you sure you followed them properly? Are you using this **2001** edition **after** 2001? (The offers in this book are good only for 2000 and 2001.) The Free Stuff Editors won't be able to send you the item, but they can make sure that any suppliers who don't fulfill requests are dropped from next year's *Free Stuff for Kids*. For **each** of your complaints, you must tell us the name of the offer as it appears in the book, the page number of the offer, and the date you sent your request. Without this information, we may not be able to help you. We'd like to know which offers you like and what kind of new offers you'd like us to add to next year's edition. So don't be bashful; write us a letter. Send your complaints or suggestions to the following address:

The Free Stuff Editors
Meadowbrook Press
5451 Smetana Drive
Minnetonka, MN 55343

Free Stuff for Kids Checklist

Use this checklist each time you send out a request. You can photocopy this page and use it again and again. It will help you follow directions **exactly** and prevent mistakes. Put a check mark in the box each time you complete a task.

For all requests,

❏ I sent my request during either 2000 or 2001.

When sending postcards and letters,

❏ I used a ballpoint pen.

❏ I printed neatly and carefully.

❏ I asked for the correct item (one only).

❏ I wrote to the correct supplier.

❏ I double-checked the supplier's address.

When sending postcards,

❏ I put my return address on the postcard.

❏ I applied a postcard stamp (if the postage wasn't preprinted).

When sending letters,

❏ I put my return address on the letter.

❏ I included a **10-inch-long self-addressed stamped envelope** (if the directions asked for one).

❏ I included the correct amount of money (if the directions asked for money).

❏ I put my return address on the upper left corner of the envelope.

❏ I put a **first-class stamp** on the envelope.

When sending a long self-addressed stamped envelope with my letter,

❏ I used a **10-inch-long envelope**.

❏ I put my address on the front of the envelope.

❏ I put my return address in the upper left corner of the envelope.

❏ I left the envelope unsealed.

❏ I applied a **first-class stamp** (or more stamps if the directions asked for more than one).

When responding to one-dollar offers,

❏ I enclosed a U.S. one-dollar bill with my letter instead of coins.

When sending coins,

❏ I sent U.S. coins.

❏ I taped the coins to my letter or to an index card.

❏ I did not stack the coins on top of each other.

❏ I did not use pennies or nickels.

Sports

Minnesota Twins

We're gonna win, Twins! You can't lose with this awesome offer from the Minnesota Twins. You'll get one fun item like a Twins player card, a schedule, or a poster of the team. Get this stuff, then get ready to cheer!

Directions:	Read and follow the instructions on pages 2-8. **Print** your name, address, and request **neatly** on a postcard.
Write to:	Minnesota Twins Attn.: Fan Relations 34 Kirby Puckett Place Minneapolis, MN 55415
Ask for:	Minnesota Twins stuff

Chicago White Sox

This offer really sox it to ya! Stick this cool White Sox logo sticker wherever you want to show your Sox pride. Don't wait! Put on your sox and shoes, run to the mailbox, and order yours today!

Directions:	Read and follow the instructions on pages 2-8. **Print** your request **neatly** on paper and put it in an envelope. You must enclose a **long self-addressed stamped envelope**.
Write to:	Chicago White Sox 333 W. 35th Street Chicago, IL 60616
Ask for:	Sox sticker

Philadelphia Phillies

If you think baseball is fabulously fun, you'll think this Philles fan pack is phenomenal. You'll receive a schedule, team photo, and two player cards—everything you need to be a fantastic Phillies fan!

Directions:	Read and follow the instructions on pages 2-8. **Print** your request **neatly** on paper and put it in an envelope. You must enclose a **long self-addressed stamped envelope**.
Write to:	Phillies P.O. Box 7575 Philadelphia, PA 19101
Ask for:	Phillies fan pack

Durham Bulls

Here's an offer that doesn't give you any bull—just great Durham Bulls stuff! You'll receive a schedule, a player card, and a card featuring the team mascot, Wool E. Bull. Charge to your mailbox and order your fan pack today!

Directions:	Read and follow the instructions on pages 2-8. **Print** your request **neatly** on paper and put it in an envelope. You must enclose a **long self-addressed stamped envelope**.
Write to:	Durham Bulls Baseball Club P.O. Box 507 Durham, NC 27702
Ask for:	Durham Bulls fan pack

San Jose Earthquakes

If you love soccer, you'll be shaking with excitement for this offer! Get this Earthquakes bumper sticker and show your solid support for a major-league soccer team that has the competition trembling.

Directions:	Read and follow the instructions on pages 2-8. **Print** your name, address, and request **neatly** on a postcard.
Write to:	San Jose Earthquakes Attn.: Customer Service Dept. Stevens Creek Boulevard, Suite 200 San Jose, CA 95117
Ask for:	Earthquakes bumper sticker

New Jersey MetroStars

Are you a super soccer fan? Then this offer will have you seeing stars—MetroStars, that is! Slap this bumper sticker wherever you want to show everyone that this soccer team is out of this world.

Directions:	Read and follow the instructions on pages 2-8. **Print** your request **neatly** on paper and put it in an envelope. You must enclose a **long self-addressed stamped envelope**.
Write to:	MetroStars Attn.: Promotions Dept. One Harmon Plaza, 3rd Floor Secaucus, NJ 07094
Ask for:	MetroStars bumper sticker

New York Islanders

The puck stops here with this great offer from the New York Islanders. You'll receive a fab fan pack that includes a player photo, sticker, schedule, and entry form for the Islanders' cool-as-ice kids' club.

Sports Cards

Can't decide whether football, basketball, baseball, or hockey is the best sport ever? You won't have to choose with this offer. You'll receive four trading cards, one for each of these four sports. Requesting these cards is an easy decision for any sports fan!

Directions:	**Read and follow the instructions on pages 2-8. Print** your name, address, and request **neatly** on a postcard.
Write to:	New York Islanders Hockey Club 1255 Hempstead Turnpike Uniondale, NY 11553
Ask for:	New York Islanders fan pack

Directions:	**Read and follow the instructions on pages 2-8. Print** your request **neatly** on paper and put it in an envelope. You must enclose a **long self-addressed stamped envelope**.
Write to:	R. Young's Quad Star Sports P.O. Box 7561 Lawton, OK 73506
Ask for:	4 free sports trading cards

Amateur Sports

Do you know what sport's best for you? Send for this info pamphlet from the Amateur Athletic Union and find out how you can get involved in organized sports.

Directions:	**Read and follow the instructions on pages 2-8. Print** your name, address, and request **neatly** on a postcard.
Write to:	Amateur Athletic Union P.O. Box 10,000 Lake Buena Vista, FL 32830
Ask for:	*AAU Sports Program* pamphlet

Wrestling

There's much more to wrestling than the wacky antics you see on TV. Wrestling is an Olympic sport that requires strength, skill, and concentration. Learn more about wrestling with this info pamphlet and decal.

Luge

This Olympic sport is as cool as ice. *Luge* means "sled" in French, and its athletes race down ice courses at speeds up to 90 miles per hour! Find out more about this sport with this info pamphlet and sticker.

Directions:	Read and follow the instructions on pages 2-8. **Print** your request **neatly** on paper and put it in an envelope. You must enclose a **long self-addressed stamped envelope**.
Write to:	USA Wrestling 6155 Lehman Drive Colorado Springs, CO 80918
Ask for:	Wrestling pamphlet and decal

Directions:	Read and follow the instructions on pages 2-8. **Print** your request **neatly** on paper and put it in an envelope. You must enclose a **long self-addressed stamped envelope**.
Write to:	USA Luge 35 Church Street Lake Placid, NY 12946
Ask for:	Luge pamphlet and sticker

USA Gymnastics

You'll flip head over heels for *Guide to Gymnastics*, a booklet that features stories about super gymnasts and information on how you can enroll in gymnastics programs. Maybe you'll become the next gymnastics phenom!

Directions:	Read and follow the instructions on pages 2-8. **Print** your name, address, and request **neatly** on a postcard.
Write to:	USA Gymnastics 201 S. Capitol Avenue Suite 300 Indianapolis, IN 46225
Ask for:	*Guide to Gymnastics* booklet

Jumping Fun

Jumping on a trampoline can be loads of fun. But getting hurt isn't any fun at all. This pamphlet teaches you how to prevent trampoline accidents and how to jump safely. Find out about trampoline safety, then bounce away to your heart's content!

Directions:	Read and follow the instructions on pages 2-8. **Print** your request **neatly** on paper and put it in an envelope. You must enclose a **long self-addressed stamped envelope**.
Write to:	The Cherry Tree 9108 Plaza Park Drive Elk Grove, CA 95624
Ask for:	Trampoline safety pamphlet

Roll On!

This skating fun pack will have you rockin' and rollin'! You'll receive a trading card and tattoo of Roooofus the Roller Roo, a trading card and tattoo of Kooky A. Bird, and a personalized letter from the wacky skating duo.

Strike!

This offer will bowl you over! You'll receive a pamphlet about bowling FUN-damentals from BIF (Bowling Is Fun), who'll teach you about choosing the right ball, following through a back swing, and scoring the game.

Directions:	Read and follow the instructions on pages 2-8. Print your request neatly on paper and put it in an envelope. You must enclose a long self-addressed stamped envelope and $1.00.
Write to:	Roller Skating Association Intl. 6905 Corporate Drive Indianapolis, IN 46278
Ask for:	Skating fun pack

Directions:	Read and follow the instructions on pages 2-8. Print your request neatly on paper and put it in an envelope. You must enclose a long self-addressed stamped envelope.
Write to:	Young American Bowling Alliance BIF and Buzzy-FB 5301 S. 76th Street Greendale, WI 53129
Ask for:	BIF's Bowling FUN-damentals pamphlet

USA Badminton

What kind of birdies can travel faster than 200 miles per hour? Badminton birdies! You can learn how to send them flying with this cool magnet. Or learn about Olympic badminton athletes with a badminton trading card.

USA BADMINTON
www.usabadminton.org
(719) 578-4808

Directions:	Read and follow the instructions on pages 2-8. Print your name, address, and request neatly on a postcard.
Write to:	USA Badminton Olympic Training Plaza One Olympic Plaza Colorado Springs, CO 80909
Ask for:	Badminton magnet or trading card

Horseshoe Rules

Learn how to pitch horseshoes like a pro. Send for this pamphlet featuring the official rules of horseshoe pitching plus a diagram showing you how to build your own regulation court.

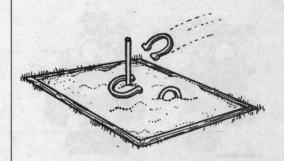

Directions:	Read and follow the instructions on pages 2-8. Print your request neatly on paper and put it in an envelope. You must enclose a long self-addressed stamped envelope.
Write to:	National Horseshoe Pitching Assn. 1721 San Ramon Way Santa Rosa, CA 95409
Ask for:	Horseshoe pitching rules

Summer Camp

School's out for the summer and you're looking for something fun to do. How about going to a cool summer camp, such as a music camp, sports camp, or just an all-around fun camp? Send for this pamphlet and find out what kind of summer camp is perfect for you.

Directions:	Read and follow the instructions on pages 2-8. Print your name, address, and request neatly on a postcard.
Write to:	American Camping Association 5000 State Road, 67 North Martinsville, IN 46151
Ask for:	*Choosing a Summer Camp* pamphlet

Paddle Fun

Don't rock the boat! Send for this pamphlet and learn how to paddle, control, and load your canoe or kayak for safe fun on the water.

Directions:	Read and follow the instructions on pages 2-8. Print your request neatly on paper and put it in an envelope. You must enclose a long self-addressed stamped envelope.
Write to:	United States Canoe Assn., Inc. P.O. Box 5743 Lafayette, IN 47903
Ask for:	*Welcome Paddler!* pamphlet

Fruity Sports Stickers

An apple playing baseball? A strawberry playing soccer? These fruits are sports nuts! You'll receive six different silly stickers featuring all kinds of fruit playing all sorts of sports.

Directions:	Read and follow the instructions on pages 2-8. **Print** your request **neatly** on paper and put it in an envelope. You must enclose a **long self-addressed stamped envelope** and **75¢**.
Write to:	Daisy Enterprises Dept. WORK P.O. Box 1426 Rutherfordton, NC 28139
Ask for:	Fruity sports stickers

Siren Whistle

Tweeeet! Time out! Stop the sports action on your school playground or in your backyard with this cool siren sports whistle. When you blow it, make sure you want to stop the game, or the players might come after you!

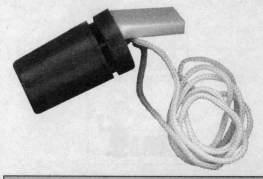

Directions:	Read and follow the instructions on pages 2-8. **Print** your request **neatly** on paper and put it in an envelope. You must enclose a **long self-addressed envelope stamped with 2 first-class stamps** and **50¢**.
Write to:	Alvin Peters Company Dept. SLWHISI P.O. Box 2050 Albany, NY 12220-0050
Ask for:	Siren whistle

Hobbies and Activities

Stamp Starter Info

Here are three pamphlets that tell you how to start a stamp collection, protect it, and find good but inexpensive stamps. With this info, you'll be in the know about this fun and exciting hobby.

Directions:	Read and follow the instructions on pages 2-8. **Print** your request **neatly** on paper and put it in an envelope. You must enclose a **long self-addressed stamped envelope.**
Write to:	American Philatelic Society P.O. Box 8000 State College, PA 16803
Ask for:	*10 Low-Cost Ways to Start Collecting Stamps, Three Tips for Stamp Collectors,* and *Welcome to Stamp Collecting!* pamphlets

Sports on Stamps

Stamp your feet and cheer for these sports on stamps. You'll receive twenty-five different canceled foreign stamps depicting such sports as sailing and cycling. See what kinds of sports different countries love enough to put on their stamps.

Directions:	Read and follow the instructions on pages 2-8. **Print** your request **neatly** on paper and put it in an envelope. You must enclose a **long self-addressed stamped envelope** and **$1.00**. *No checks, please.*
Write to:	Universal P.O. Box 226FSP Port Washington, NY 11050-0226
Ask for:	Sports on stamps

Awesome Offer

U.S. Christmas Stamps

Ho! Ho! Ho! 'Tis the season for stamp collectors. You'll receive twenty different canceled U.S. Christmas stamps, each one depicting a scene of holiday cheer. This is a jolly offer for any stamp collector.

Directions:	Read and follow the instructions on pages 2-8. Print your request neatly on paper and put it in an envelope. You must enclose a long self-addressed stamped envelope and $1.00. *No checks, please.*
Write to:	J. Alexander Dept. XM P.O. Box 213 Roslyn, NY 11576-0213
Ask for:	20 canceled U.S. Christmas Stamps

Fifty Stamps

This offer is a terrific way to start a collection and to see the U.S.A.! You'll receive fifty different canceled United States stamps, each one featuring a picture depicting American life.

Directions:	Read and follow the instructions on pages 2-8. Print your request neatly on paper and put it in an envelope. You must enclose a long self-addressed stamped envelope and $1.00. *No checks, please.*
Write to:	J. Alexander Dept. CS P.O. Box 7 Roslyn, NY 11576-0007
Ask for:	50 canceled U.S. stamps

Coins

Ever wonder what coins countries like Finland, Brazil, Turkey, Cyprus, or Israel use? You'll know if you order these cool foreign coins, one from each of these five countries. None is currently circulating, so get yours today before they're gone forever.

Directions:	Read and follow the instructions on pages 2-8. Print your request neatly on paper and put it in an envelope. You must enclose a long self-addressed envelope stamped with 2 first-class stamps and $1.00. *No checks, please.*
Write to:	Jolie Coins Dept. FSB P.O. Box 399 Roslyn Heights, NY 11577-0399
Ask for:	Foreign coins

Bank Notes

You won't need to travel to another country to receive these five genuine colorful bank notes, two from Indonesia and one each from Peru, Great Britain, and Brazil. Order yours today and they'll travel to you!

Directions:	Read and follow the instructions on pages 2-8. Print your request neatly on paper and put it in an envelope. You must enclose a long self-addressed stamped envelope and $1.00. *No checks, please.*
Write to:	Jolie Coins Dept. FS P.O. Box 399 Roslyn Heights, NY 11577-0399
Ask for:	Foreign bank notes

Buffalo Nickel

Did you know that over fifty years ago nickels used to feature buffaloes? Don't believe it? Well, order your buffalo nickel today to start or add to your coin collection.

Mercury Dime

From 1916–1945, dimes bore the image of Mercury, the Roman god of commerce and travel. Now Mercury dimes are rare—in fact, they're considered collectors' items. Add one to your collection!

Directions:	Read and follow the instructions on pages 2-8. Print your request neatly on paper and put it in an envelope. You must enclose a long self-addressed stamped envelope and 50¢. No checks, please.
Write to:	Edinboro Creations Dept. BUF 1210 Brierly Lane Munhall, PA 15120
Ask for:	One buffalo nickel

Directions:	Read and follow the instructions on pages 2-8. Print your request neatly on paper and put it in an envelope. You must enclose a long self-addressed stamped envelope and $1.00. No checks, please.
Write to:	Edinboro Creations Dept. MER 1210 Brierly Lane Munhall, PA 15120
Ask for:	One mercury dime

Macramé Choker & Bracelet

This kit has everything you need to make a fabulous beaded macramé choker and bracelet, including easy-to-follow instructions. This jewelry is way cool, and making it is a perfect activity any day of the year.

Safety Pin Bracelet

How much fun could you have with some beads, safety pins, and elastic string? A lot! But only if you order this cool, colorful beaded safety pin bracelet kit. You'll get all the materials and easy-to-follow directions.

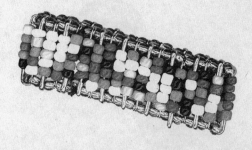

Directions:	**Read and follow the instructions on pages 2-8. Print** your request **neatly** on paper and put it in an envelope. You must enclose a **long self-addressed envelope stamped with 2 first-class stamps** and **$1.00**.
Write to:	Little Angels Crafts 1423 Dayton Street Coquitlam, BC V3E 3H2 Canada
Ask for:	Macramé choker and bracelet kit

Directions:	**Read and follow the instructions on pages 2-8. Print** your request **neatly** on paper and put it in an envelope. You must enclose a **long self-addressed envelope stamped with 2 first-class stamps** and **$1.00**.
Write to:	Grin 'N' Barrett Dept. SP 1227 S. Muirfield Road Los Angeles, CA 90019-3040
Ask for:	Beaded safety pin bracelet kit

Birthstone Buddies

Did you know every month has its own special stone? You can make a necklace with a boy or girl charm that has a center the same color as your own birthstone. Kit includes materials and easy-to-follow instructions.

Directions:	Read and follow the instructions on pages 2-8. Print your request neatly on paper and put it in an envelope. You must enclose a long self-addressed stamped envelope and $1.00.
Write to:	Grin 'N' Barrett Dept. BS 1227 S. Muirfield Road Los Angeles, CA 90019-3040
Ask for:	Birthstone buddies charm necklace kit (Specify birthday month.)

Daisy Chain Bracelet

Need a great gift for your best friend's birthday? Something special to wear with your new outfit? This cute, colorful, beaded daisy chain bracelet is perfect for you or a friend and is lots of fun to make. Kit includes materials and easy-to-follow directions.

Directions:	Read and follow the instructions on pages 2-8. Print your request neatly on paper and put it in an envelope. You must enclose a long self-addressed envelope stamped with 2 first-class stamps and $1.00.
Write to:	Little Angels Crafts 1423 Dayton Street Coquitlam, BC V3E 3H2 Canada
Ask for:	Daisy chain bracelet bead kit

Origami

Origami is the cool art of paper folding. With these two fun books, learn how to create an entire zoo or a whole set of Christmas decorations just by folding ordinary sheets of paper! You can order one of the books or both at the same time.

Directions:	**Read and follow the instructions on pages 2-8. Print** your name, address, and request **neatly** on paper and put it in an envelope. You must enclose **$1.00 for each book.**
Write to:	Winslow Publishing P.O. Box 38012 Toronto, ON M5N 3A8 Canada
Ask for:	Animals origami book **or** Christmas origami book **or** both origami books

Rain Forest Poster

Design your own special rain forest scene with this awesome rain forest poster kit. You'll receive six sheets of bugs, birds, frogs, lizards, lemurs, and other jungle critters to cut out and paste on a colorful background sheet.

Directions:	**Read and follow the instructions on pages 2-8. Print** your name, address, and request **neatly** on paper and put it in an envelope. You must enclose **$1.00.**
Write to:	Winslow Publishing P.O. Box 38012 Toronto, ON M5N 3A8 Canada
Ask for:	Rain forest poster kit

Wacky Masks and Hats

Would you wear a silly frog hat? How about a spooky ghost mask? These are just two goofy things you can make from ordinary paper plates. You'll receive three different easy-to-follow patterns plus a packet of glitter to decorate your creations.

Directions:	Read and follow the instructions on pages 2-8. Print your request neatly on paper and put it in an envelope. You must enclose a long self-addressed stamped envelope and 75¢.
Write to:	Grin 'N' Barrett Dept. HM 1227 S. Muirfield Road Los Angeles, CA 90019-3040
Ask for:	Masks and hats kit

Zoo Animal

Create your own cuddly zoo animal with this fun kit. You'll receive one of the following easy-to-make zoo animals: zebra, elephant, tiger, or lion. Kit includes materials and loads of fun!

Directions:	Read and follow the instructions on pages 2-8. Print your request neatly on paper and put it in an envelope. You must enclose a long self-addressed envelope stamped with 2 first-class stamps and 50¢.
Write to:	McVehil's Mercantile Dept. MPZA One Rasel Avenue Washington, PA 15301
Ask for:	Zoo animal kit

Watercolors

Are you a budding artist? Do you love to paint? You can mix up your own cakes of watercolor paint with this offer. You'll receive instructions to make the paint plus a paintbrush to get you started creating your own masterpieces.

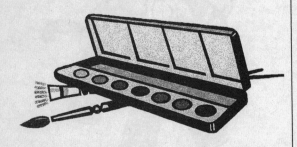

Directions:	Read and follow the instructions on **pages 2-8. Print** your request **neatly** on paper and put it in an envelope. You must enclose a **long self-addressed stamped envelope** and **25¢**. *No checks, please.*
Write to:	The Painting Gorilla 1210 Commonwealth Avenue Munhall, PA 15120
Ask for:	Wonderful watercolors

Animal Paper

Make wild cutouts, stationery, or wrapping paper with this cool animal-print craft paper. You'll receive five different sheets printed with furry and feathery animal designs.

Directions:	Read and follow the instructions on **pages 2-8. Print** your name, address, and request **neatly** on paper and put it in an envelope. You must enclose **$1.00**.
Write to:	Winslow Publishing P.O. Box 38012 Toronto, ON M5N 3A8 Canada
Ask for:	Animal craft paper

Stationery Set

Share some smiles with all your pen pals by using this smiley-face stationery set. You bring the paper and envelope; this offer will provide the pencils, erasers, and stickers. Start writing!

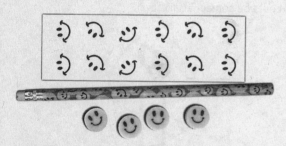

Address Labels

Slap these labels on your letters to friends, pen pals, or family. Use them for your *Free Stuff for Kids* requests. You'll get thirty labels featuring your name, your address, and a cool design. Choose from cat and dog, shark, peace symbol, galaxy, smiley faces and stars, or dinosaur designs.

Megan McGinnis
Meadowbrook Press
5451 Smetana Drive
Minnetonka, MN 55343

Directions:	Read and follow the instructions on pages 2-8. Print your request neatly on paper and put it in an envelope. You must enclose a long self-addressed stamped envelope and 75¢. *No checks, please.*
Write to:	Edinboro Creations Dept. P 1210 Brierly Lane Munhall, PA 15120
Ask for:	Smiley-face stationery set

Directions:	Read and follow the instructions on pages 2-8. Print your request neatly on paper and put it in an envelope. You must enclose a long self-addressed stamped envelope and $1.00.
Write to:	Daisy Enterprises Dept. LAB P.O. Box 1426 Rutherfordton, NC 28139
Ask for:	Address labels (Specify **one** design **and** print your name and address neatly.)

Fan Club Addresses

Are you your favorite star's biggest fan? Write a letter and let that celebrity know how you feel. You'll receive one hundred fan club addresses for stars like Mariah Carey, *NSYNC, Cal Ripken Jr., Tara Lipinski, and many more.

Directions:	Read and follow the instructions on pages 2-8. **Print** your request **neatly** on paper and put it in an envelope. You must enclose a **long self-addressed stamped envelope** and **50¢**.
Write to:	Special Products Dept. A 3427 Burks Court Bloomington, IN 47401
Ask for:	100 fan club addresses

Write for Rights

Writing a letter could save someone's life. Help people around the globe who are imprisoned, hurt, or worse by receiving the Children's Edition Urgent Action pack. You'll get stickers, games, info on kids in danger, and instructions on writing a letter that could be someone's lifesaver.

Directions:	Read and follow the instructions on pages 2-8. **Print** your name, address, and request **neatly** on a postcard
Write to:	Amnesty International USA Children's Edition Urgent Action P.O. Box 1270 Nederland, CO 80466-1270
Ask for:	Children's Edition UA pack

World Pen Pals

Curious how kids around the world live? You can learn the answer to this question and more by filling out this application for a pen friend from any continent except Australia. You could be starting a friendship that crosses an ocean!

WORLD PEN PALS
P.O. Box 337
Saugerties, NY 12477 USA

Pen Pals

Want to meet a friend across the country or across the sea? You can if you send for this application form and start the process to get connected to a new pen friend. This is a great way to meet people and have lots of fun!

Directions:	Read and follow the instructions on pages 2-8. **Print** your request **neatly** on paper and put it in an envelope. You must enclose a **long self-addressed stamped envelope**.
Write to:	World Pen Pals P.O. Box 337 Saugerties, NY 12477
Ask for:	World Pen Pal application

Directions:	Read and follow the instructions on pages 2-8. **Print** your request **neatly** on paper and put it in an envelope. You must enclose a **long self-addressed stamped envelope**.
Write to:	Forever Friendship Dept. MP-INFO P.O. Box 1072 Monticello, MN 55362
Ask for:	Personalized pen pal connection

FREE

GAMES

Check Out Chess

Learn to play chess like a grand master—or simply learn how to play the game—with this info. You'll get a booklet that features ten tips on how to improve your chess game and the pamphlet *Let's Play Chess,* which explains how this great game works.

Mini Activity Pad

Whether you're traveling by car or school bus, this activity pad will make the travel time fly by. It's full of fun games like hangman, tic-tac-toe, and many others. You'll receive one mini activity pad for lots of entertainment.

Directions:	Read and follow the instructions on pages 2-8. **Print** your request **neatly** on paper and put it in an envelope. You must enclose a **long self-addressed stamped envelope.**
Write to:	U.S. Chess Federation Dept. 26 3054 NYS Route 9W New Windsor, NY 12553
Ask for:	*Ten Tips to Winning Chess* booklet and *Let's Play Chess* pamphlet

Directions:	Read and follow the instructions on pages 2-8. **Print** your request **neatly** on paper and put it in an envelope. You must enclose a **long self-addressed stamped envelope** and **35¢.**
Write to:	Daisy Enterprises Dept. AP P.O. Box 1426 Rutherfordton, NC 28139
Ask for:	Travel mini activity pad

Toys and Other Fun Stuff

Dino Gliders

Fly these easy-to-assemble gliders and see how winged dinosaurs might have soared through the air. You'll receive two different Styrofoam dinosaur gliders perfect for flying outdoors or indoors.

Directions:	Read and follow the instructions on pages 2-8. **Print** your name, address, and request **neatly** on paper and put it in an envelope. You must enclose **$1.00**.
Write to:	Neetstuff Dept. FS-71 P.O. Box 353 Rio Grande, NJ 08242
Ask for:	Dino gliders

Take Flight!

Cruise the skies with this fun star glider and soaring jet. Both are easy to put together. You're sure to have hours of high-flying fun with this offer!

Directions:	Read and follow the instructions on pages 2-8. **Print** your request **neatly** on paper and put it in an envelope. You must enclose a **long self-addressed stamped envelope** and **50¢**.
Write to:	The Cherry Tree 9108 Plaza Park Drive Elk Grove, CA 95624
Ask for:	Star glider and soaring jet

STICKY STUFF

Sticky Feet

This offer will really stick with you. Be careful where you fling these two sticky feet, though. They'll stick to nearly everything they touch: your friend's homework, your mom's favorite vase, or even your little brother's hair!

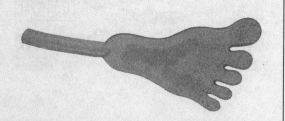

Directions:	Read and follow the instructions on pages 2-8. Print your request neatly on paper and put it in an envelope. You must enclose a long self-addressed envelope stamped with 2 first-class stamps and 75¢.
Write to:	Alvin Peters Company Dept. CASTFOO P.O. Box 2050 Albany, NY 12220-0050
Ask for:	Sticky feet

Sticky Bug

Throw this sticky-footed bug against a wall or window and watch it slowly tumble down end over end. The bug features a face like an alien face or a smiley face.

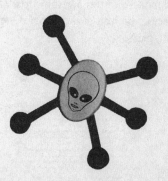

Directions:	Read and follow the instructions on pages 2-8. Print your request neatly on paper and put it in an envelope. You must enclose a long self-addressed envelope stamped with 2 first-class stamps and 75¢.
Write to:	Alvin Peters Company Dept. NB4693 P.O. Box 2050 Albany, NY 12220-0050
Ask for:	Tumble-down-the-walls bug

First Name Almanac

What does your first name mean? What's its history? What are its interesting characteristics? Learn all this and more with this awesome first name almanac printed on high-quality paper. One name per request, please.

Birthday Chronicle

Extra! Extra! Give your first and last names plus your birthdate including year and learn what celebrities share your birthday, what the top songs, movies, and sports events were, plus much more!

Directions:	Read and follow the instructions on pages 2-8. **Print** your request **neatly** on paper and put it in an envelope. You must enclose a **long self-addressed stamped envelope** and **$1.00.**
Write to:	Special Products Dept. F 3427 Burks Court Bloomington, IN 47401
Ask for:	First name almanac (Print your name neatly.)

Directions:	Read and follow the instructions on pages 2-8. **Print** your request **neatly** on paper and put it in an envelope. You must enclose a **long self-addressed stamped envelope** and **$1.00.**
Write to:	Special Products Dept. B 3427 Burks Court Bloomington, IN 47401
Ask for:	Birthday chronicle (Print your first and last names neatly **and** specify your birthdate.)

Spiral Stencils

Spin these wheels and you'll end up with some way-cool art! These stencils come in assorted tropical designs and have two spiral wheels you can turn round and round with a pen or pencil to create beautiful designs. You'll receive one stencil.

Directions: **Read and follow the instructions on pages 2-8. Print** your request **neatly** on paper and put it in an envelope. You must enclose a **long self-addressed stamped envelope** and **50¢**. *No checks, please.*

Write to: Lauren & Company
Dept. TSS
P.O. Box 1019
Mundelein, IL 60060

Ask for: Tropical spiral stencil

Glowing Tracers

You can have fun two different ways with these eight out-of-this-world tracers. Use them to trace a galaxy onto anything that's earthbound. Or stick them on your walls or ceiling, turn out the lights, and watch them glow in the dark.

Directions: **Read and follow the instructions on pages 2-8. Print** your request **neatly** on paper and put it in an envelope. You must enclose a **long self-addressed envelope, stamped with 2 first-class stamps** and **50¢.**

Write to: The Cherry Tree
9108 Plaza Park Drive
Elk Grove, CA 95624

Ask for: Glow-in-the-dark planets

Tic-Tac-Toe

Now you can play tic-tac-toe wherever you go with this pocket game on a key ring. Whether you're riding on the school bus or waiting in line for a movie, you and a friend can pass the time playing this fun game.

Stretchy Lizard

Pull this lizard as far as it'll go. Stretch it for all it's worth. Go on! This lizard can take it. You'll receive one colorful, realistic-looking lizard for hours of pulling and stretching fun.

Directions:	**Read and follow the instructions on pages 2-8. Print** your request **neatly** on paper and put it in an envelope. You must enclose a **long self-addressed envelope stamped with 2 first-class stamps** and **75¢**.
Write to:	Alvin Peters Company Dept. NB4932 P.O. Box 2050 Albany, NY 12220-0050
Ask for:	Pocket tic-tac-toe game

Directions:	**Read and follow the instructions on pages 2-8. Print** your request **neatly** on paper and put it in an envelope. You must enclose a **long self-addressed stamped envelope** and **$1.00**.
Write to:	Daisy Enterprises Dept. SLRD P.O. Box 1426 Rutherfordton, NC 28139
Ask for:	Stretchy lizard

Critter Patch

What's that crawling on you? A bug? A salamander? Oh wait, that's your cool, new critter iron-on patch! You'll receive one of these creatures to iron onto your favorite shirt, pair of jeans, or anything else made of fabric.

Directions:	Read and follow the instructions on pages 2-8. **Print** your request **neatly** on paper and put it in an envelope. You must enclose a **long self-addressed stamped envelope** and **$1.00**.
Write to:	Daisy Enterprises Dept. CTRP P.O. Box 1426 Rutherfordton, NC 28139
Ask for:	Critter iron-on patch

Rub-Ons

Rub a bit of nature onto your mirror, window, or favorite mug. These butterfly and flower rub-ons can be transferred onto almost any flat surface. You'll receive one sheet of assorted butterfly and flower rub-ons.

Directions:	Read and follow the instructions on pages 2-8. **Print** your request **neatly** on paper and put it in an envelope. You must enclose a **long self-addressed stamped envelope** and **$1.00**.
Write to:	Alvin Peters Company Dept. NB4747 P.O. Box 2050 Albany, NY 12220-0050
Ask for:	Butterfly and flower rub-ons

Neon Shoelaces

Make a fashion statement with these neon shoelaces. The bright colors are sure to draw attention to your feet, so even if your sneakers aren't flashy, your shoelaces certainly will be! You'll receive one pair of neon shoelaces.

Directions:	Read and follow the instructions on pages 2-8. **Print** your request **neatly** on paper and put it in an envelope. You must enclose a **long self-addressed stamped envelope** and **75¢**. *No checks, please.*
Write to:	The Goody Box P.O. Box 400 Scurry, TX 75158
Ask for:	Neon shoelaces

Shoelace Charm

This offer will charm you. You'll receive one gold-toned shoelace charm with a clasp to hook it onto your shoelace bow, backpack, or necklace. Charm comes in assorted styles like a guitar or a teddy bear.

Directions:	Read and follow the instructions on pages 2-8. **Print** your request **neatly** on paper and put it in an envelope. You must enclose a **long self-addressed stamped envelope** and **75¢**.
Write to:	Daisy Enterprises Dept. CHARM P.O. Box 1426 Rutherfordton, NC 28139
Ask for:	Shoelace charm

Awesome Offer

Bike-Spoke Charms

Ride your bike in style with these cool bicycle-spoke charms. You'll receive one set of four colorful charms, each with a reflective center, to snap onto the spokes of your bike.

Directions:	Read and follow the instructions on pages 2-8. **Print** your request **neatly** on paper and put it in an envelope. You must enclose a **long self-addressed stamped envelope** and **75¢**.
Write to:	Daisy Enterprises Dept. BSC P.O. Box 1426 Rutherfordton, NC 28139
Ask for:	Bicycle-spoke charms

Surprise Stuff

If you love surprises, this offer won't disappoint you! You'll receive one of the following items: cool stickers, funky animal comb, adorable book clip, or another great item. We can't tell you more because it's a surprise!

Directions:	Read and follow the instructions on pages 2-8. **Print** your request **neatly** on paper and put it in an envelope. You must enclose a **long self-addressed stamped envelope** and **25¢**. *No checks, please.*
Write to:	Edinboro Creations Dept. A 1210 Brierly Lane Munhall, PA 15120
Ask for:	Surprise stuff

Paper Doll Stickers

Change fashions instantly with these paper doll stickers. Easily apply and remove the cool clothes and accessories as many times as you want. You'll receive one sheet of paper doll stickers including 2 dolls and assorted outfits.

Directions:	Read and follow the instructions on pages 2-8. **Print** your request **neatly** on paper and put it in an envelope. You must enclose a **long self-addressed stamped envelope** and **$1.00**.
Write to:	Winslow Publishing P.O. Box 38012 Toronto, Ontario M5N 3A8 Canada
Ask for:	Paper doll stickers

Flower Coin Pouch

Get more power from your coin pouch—flower power, that is! This colorful pouch, decorated with smiling flowers, can hold a lot more than just your change. The key ring makes it easy to hook onto your backpack, belt loop, or wherever.

Directions:	Read and follow the instructions on pages 2-8. **Print** your request **neatly** on paper and put it in an envelope. You must enclose a **long self-addressed stamped envelope** and **$1.00**.
Write to:	Phil Labush 9360 NW 39th Street Sunrise, FL 33351
Ask for:	Flower coin pouch

Lucky Coin Pouch

How lucky you'll feel if you get this adorable coin pouch to carry your change! You'll receive a pouch in one of the following zoo animal designs: tiger, monkey, zebra, elephant, or giraffe. Each cute pouch has lucky penny inside to get your good luck started.

Directions:	Read and follow the instructions on pages 2-8. Print your request neatly on paper and put it in an envelope. You must enclose a long self-addressed stamped envelope and $1.00. *No checks, please.*
Write to:	Sarah's Treasures 1210 Commonwealth Avenue Munhall, PA 15120
Ask for:	Zoo animal lucky coin pouch

Fish Coin Pouch

Nothing fishy about this offer. It's fin-tastic! You'll receive one brightly colored leather fish coin pouch to hold your coins and much more.

Directions:	Read and follow the instructions on pages 2-8. Print your request neatly on paper and put it in an envelope. You must enclose a long self-addressed envelope stamped with 2 first-class stamps and 75¢.
Write to:	McVehil's Mercantile Dept. MPLF One Rasel Avenue Washington, PA 15301
Ask for:	Fish coin pouch

Frog Necklace

Frogs are said to bring good luck, so if you want some good luck of your own, this necklace is for you. You'll receive one frog paua shell charm on a long black cord. Hop to your mailbox and order one today!

Jelly Bracelets and Rings

Can anyone have too much glittery jewelry? No way! The more, the better! With this offer, you'll receive four glitter jelly bracelets and two glitter jelly rings, all in assorted colors. Wear them all yourself or share them with a friend.

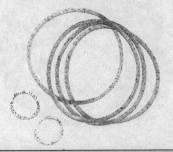

Directions:	Read and follow the instructions on pages 2-8. **Print** your request **neatly** on paper and put it in an envelope. You must enclose a **long self-addressed stamped envelope** and **$1.00**.
Write to:	Phil Labush 9360 NW 39th Street Sunrise, FL 33351
Ask for:	Frog paua shell necklace

Directions:	Read and follow the instructions on pages 2-8. **Print** your request **neatly** on paper and put it in an envelope. You must enclose a **long self-addressed stamped envelope** and **$1.00**.
Write to:	Daisy Enterprises Dept. JELLY P.O. Box 1426 Rutherfordton, NC 28139
Ask for:	Glitter jelly bracelets and rings

Ear Cuff Charm

Now hear this! Earrings aren't the only jewelry your lobes can sport. This ear cuff with cool charm will also make your ears look fashionable. You'll receive one ear cuff with a charm like a heart, peace symbol, or another awesome design.

Directions:	Read and follow the instructions on pages 2-8. **Print** your request **neatly** on paper and put it in an envelope. You must enclose a **long self-addressed stamped envelope** and **$1.00**.
Write to:	Daisy Enterprises Dept. EB P.O. Box 1426 Rutherfordton, NC 28139
Ask for:	Ear cuff charm

Heart-Drop Necklace

Yee haw! This is a knee-slappin' good offer! This hand-beaded necklace with a brightly colored heart charm combines Old West style with today's fashions. You'll receive one rootin' tootin' good-lookin' necklace.

Directions:	Read and follow the instructions on pages 2-8. **Print** your request **neatly** on paper and put it in an envelope. You must enclose a **long self-addressed stamped envelope** and **$1.00**.
Write to:	Grin 'N' Barrett Dept. HD 1227 S. Muirfield Road Los Angeles, CA 90019-3040
Ask for:	Heart-drop lariat necklace

"Tattoo" Necklace & Bracelet

We're not stretching the truth. This cool stretchy beaded necklace and bracelet will make you look as if you have colorful, intricate designs tattooed around your neck and wrist. No lie!

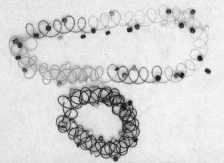

Directions:	Read and follow the instructions on pages 2-8. **Print** your request **neatly** on paper and put it in an envelope. You must enclose a **long self-addressed stamped envelope** and **$1.00**.
Write to:	Daisy Enterprises Dept. NB P.O. Box 1426 Rutherfordton, NC 28139
Ask for:	Stretchy "tattoo" necklace and bracelet set

Nail Decals

Who needs messy nail polish when you can have these fantastic glitter nail decals to dress up your fingertips? You'll receive one pack of thirty-five decals in fun designs like butterflies, hearts, and roses.

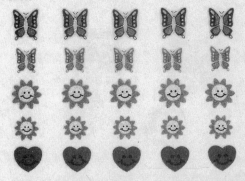

Directions:	Read and follow the instructions on pages 2-8. **Print** your request **neatly** on paper and put it in an envelope. You must enclose a **long self-addressed stamped envelope** and **$1.00**.
Write to:	Daisy Enterprises Dept. GND P.O. Box 1426 Rutherfordton, NC 28139
Ask for:	Glitter nail decals

Stickers and Tattoos

Baby Animals

Is there anything cuter than these sweet-faced baby animal stickers? Probably not! You'll receive five different stickers, each measuring over 2 by 2 inches. How could anyone resist this adorable offer?

Directions:	Read and follow the instructions on pages 2-8. Print your request neatly on paper and put it in an envelope. You must enclose a long self-addressed stamped envelope and 75¢.
Write to:	Daisy Enterprises Dept. ANBS P.O. Box 1426 Rutherfordton, NC 28139
Ask for:	Baby animal stickers

Riddles

Q: Why did the kid cross the road?
A: To get these silly riddle stickers, of course! You'll receive five different stickers. Each features a fun, colorful picture and a hilarious riddle. You'll have everyone giggling with these wacky stickers!

Directions:	Read and follow the instructions on pages 2-8. Print your request neatly on paper and put it in an envelope. You must enclose a long self-addressed stamped envelope and 75¢.
Write to:	Daisy Enterprises Dept. RIDS P.O. Box 1426 Rutherfordton, NC 28139
Ask for:	Riddle stickers

Puffy Dinosaurs

These dinosaurs are the cheeriest reptiles you'll ever meet! You'll receive three colorful puffy stickers that are sure to stand out in any sticker collection.

Directions:	Read and follow the instructions on pages 2-8. Print your request neatly on paper and put it in an envelope. You must enclose a long self-addressed stamped envelope and 50¢.
Write to:	Daisy Enterprises Dept. PDS P.O. Box 1426 Rutherfordton, NC 28139
Ask for:	Puffy dinosaur stickers

Dinostickers

Dinosaurs no longer exist, but this offer keeps them alive. You'll receive five different stickers that feature dinosaurs like tyrannosaurus rex, stegosaurus, or velociraptor. Order today before this offer becomes extinct.

Directions:	Read and follow the instructions on pages 2-8. Print your request neatly on paper and put it in an envelope. You must enclose a long self-addressed stamped envelope and 75¢.
Write to:	Daisy Enterprises Dept. DINOS P.O. Box 1426 Rutherfordton, NC 28139
Ask for:	Dinostickers

Monster Trucks

These trucks may be monsters, but there's nothing scary about this offer. You'll receive four different cool monster truck stickers. Can't you almost hear their big, bad engines revvin'?

Jet Fighters

This offer will send you soaring into the skies. You'll receive five different stickers featuring awesome jet fighter planes. Hurry and order yours today so you can take flight!

Directions:	Read and follow the instructions on pages 2-8. **Print** your request **neatly** on paper and put it in an envelope. You must enclose a **long self-addressed stamped envelope** and **75¢**.
Write to:	Daisy Enterprises Dept. MOTS P.O. Box 1426 Rutherfordton, NC 28139
Ask for:	Monster truck stickers

Directions:	Read and follow the instructions on pages 2-8. **Print** your request **neatly** on paper and put it in an envelope. You must enclose a **long self-addressed stamped envelope** and **75¢**.
Write to:	Daisy Enterprises Dept. JETS P.O. Box 1426 Rutherfordton, NC 28139
Ask for:	Jet fighter stickers

Smiley Faces

You're sure to smile if you order this offer. You'll receive twenty colorful smiley-face stickers, both round and heart-shaped. Stick them anyplace you want to flash a smile.

Best Friends

Here's a terrific way to make friendships stick. You'll receive one sheet of stickers to show every-one just how tight you and your best buds are.

Directions:	Read and follow the instructions on pages 2-8. Print your request neatly on paper and put it in an envelope. You must enclose a long self-addressed stamped envelope and 50¢.
Write to:	Fax Marketing Dept. 2001 460 Carrollton Drive Frederick, MD 21701
Ask for:	Smiley-face stickers

Directions:	Read and follow the instructions on pages 2-8. Print your request neatly on paper and put it in an envelope. You must enclose a long self-addressed stamped envelope and 50¢.
Write to:	Alvin Peters Company Dept. 9604 P.O. Box 2050 Albany, NY 12220-0050
Ask for:	Best friends stickers

Fuzzy Stickers

You'll feel warm and fuzzy inside with these colorful fuzzy stickers. A pig, troll doll, elephant, and lion are just four of the twenty-four cute fuzzy stickers you'll receive with this heartwarming offer.

Itty-Bitty Stickers

You'll get so many of these jewel-colored itty-bitty stickers you won't know what to do. Decorate your fingernails, earlobes, or anything else you want to perk up. You'll receive two sheets of seventy stickers in assorted shapes like cats, fish, and teddy bears.

Directions:	Read and follow the instructions on pages 2-8. **Print** your request **neatly** on paper and put it in an envelope. You must enclose a **long self-addressed stamped envelope** and **$1.00**.
Write to:	Stickers 'N' Stuff Dept. FZ24 P.O. Box 430 Louisville, CO 80027
Ask for:	24 fuzzy stickers

Directions:	Read and follow the instructions on pages 2-8. **Print** your request **neatly** on paper and put it in an envelope. You must enclose a **long self-addressed stamped envelope** and **$1.00**.
Write to:	Stickers 'N' Stuff Dept. Itty-2 P.O. Box 430 Louisville, CO 80027
Ask for:	140 itty-bitty stickers

Touch Me! Stickers

These foamie stickers are *soooo* cool! When you touch them, they change colors right before your eyes. With this one fantastic offer, you'll receive two glittery foamie stickers shaped like dolphins, castles, monkeys, butterflies, suns, moons, or one of many other shapes.

Directions:	Read and follow the instructions on pages 2-8. **Print** your request **neatly** on paper and put it in an envelope. You must enclose a **long self-addressed stamped envelope** and **$1.00**. *No checks, please.*
Write to:	Edinboro Creations Dept. TM 1210 Brierly Lane Munhall, PA 15120
Ask for:	Touch Me! foamie stickers

Scratch and Sniff

These stickers have lots of smell appeal! You'll receive one sheet of at least twelve scratch-and-sniff stickers. Sticker sheets come in assorted designs and give off scrumptious smells like root beer, bubble gum, pizza, and cotton candy.

Directions:	Read and follow the instructions on pages 2-8. **Print** your request **neatly** on paper and put it in an envelope. You must enclose a **long self-addressed envelope (no stamp required)** and **$1.00**.
Write to:	The Very Best Sticker Company Dept. HOLI P.O. Box 3063 Barrington, IL 60011
Ask for:	Scratch-and-sniff sticker sheet

Unicorns

Take the magic of unicorns with you wherever you go with these spectacular unicorn stickers. You'll receive four different stickers featuring these enchanting animals on a background of shiny silver stars.

Directions:	Read and follow the instructions on pages 2-8. Print your request neatly on paper and put it in an envelope. You must enclose a long self-addressed stamped envelope and 50¢.
Write to:	Daisy Enterprises Dept. MUNS P.O. Box 1426 Rutherfordton, NC 28139
Ask for:	Mylar unicorn stickers

Looney Tunes

What's up, doc? These five cool laser stickers featuring some of your favorite Looney Tunes characters such as Bugs Bunny, Taz, Sylvester, and Tweety—that's what! Sufferin' succotash! This is a great offer!

Directions:	Read and follow the instructions on pages 2-8. Print your request neatly on paper and put it in an envelope. You must enclose a long self-addressed stamped envelope and $1.00.
Write to:	Daisy Enterprises Dept. LLTS P.O. Box 1426 Rutherfordton, NC 28139
Ask for:	Laser Looney Tunes stickers

Bugs

If you love creepy crawlies, you're sure to go buggy for these bug tattoos! You'll receive one pack of eight or more tattoos of flies, moths, centipedes, and other bugs.

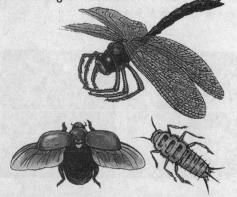

Critters

Don't let these tattoos bug you. You'll want to have these creepy, crawly critters on your arm or leg. You'll receive four different insect and amphibian tattoos featuring such colorful creatures as salamanders, frogs, and dragonflies.

Directions:	Read and follow the instructions on pages 2-8. Print your request neatly on paper and put it in an envelope. You must enclose a long self-addressed stamped envelope and $1.00.
Write to:	B Mom's Dept. BUG 169 North Main Street Rutherfordton, NC 28139
Ask for:	Bug tattoos

Directions:	Read and follow the instructions on pages 2-8. Print your request neatly on paper and put it in an envelope. You must enclose a long self-addressed stamped envelope and 50¢.
Write to:	Daisy Enterprises Dept. IRT2 P.O. Box 1426 Rutherfordton, NC 28139
Ask for:	Critter tattoos

Butterflies

With these detailed, colorful butterfly tattoos, you'll have people wondering if your mom or dad let you get a real tattoo! You'll receive a sheet of more than eight glittery butterfly tattoos sure to fool anyone into thinking you've gotten the real thing.

Directions:	Read and follow the instructions on pages 2-8. Print your request neatly on paper and put it in an envelope. You must enclose a long self-addressed stamped envelope and $1.00.
Write to:	Winslow Publishing P.O. Box 38012 Toronto, Ontario M5N 3A8 Canada
Ask for:	Glitter butterfly tattoos

Superman!

Okay, these Superman tattoos won't make you move faster than a speeding bullet or leap tall buildings in single bound. But they will make you feel super! You'll receive five tattoos featuring different designs of the Man of Steel.

Directions:	Read and follow the instructions on pages 2-8. Print your request neatly on paper and put it in an envelope. You must enclose a long self-addressed stamped envelope and $1.00.
Write to:	Daisy Enterprises Dept. SPMT P.O. Box 1426 Rutherfordton, NC 28139
Ask for:	Superman tattoos

Hand Tattoos

Here's a handy way to decorate your entire hand. This pack of bright tattoos has forty different styles to adorn your fingernails, wrists, and everywhere in between. What a terrific offer!

Ring Tattoos

This tattoo offer will be wrapped around your finger—or your toe, if you like. You'll receive one pack of seven cool ring tattoos to wear around your fingers or toes. Wherever you decide to put them, you'll be in style!

Directions:	**Read and follow the instructions on pages 2-8. Print** your request **neatly** on paper and put it in an envelope. You must enclose a **long self-addressed stamped envelope** and **$1.00**.
Write to:	Daisy Enterprises Dept. HAND P.O. Box 1426 Rutherfordton, NC 28139
Ask for:	Pack of hand tattoos

Directions:	**Read and follow the instructions on pages 2-8. Print** your request **neatly** on paper and put it in an envelope. You must enclose a **long self-addressed stamped envelope** and **$1.00**.
Write to:	Daisy Enterprises Dept. RTAT P.O. Box 1426 Rutherfordton, NC 28139
Ask for:	Ring tattoos

Bellybutton Tattoos

Bellybutton tattoos aren't just for bellybuttons anymore. You can wear these four tattoos, each with a different colorful design, anywhere you want to look groovy.

Wrist Tattoos

Everyone will be green with envy when they see one of these colorful tattoos wrapped around your wrist or ankle. You'll receive two tattoos in awesome designs, such as sharks or roses. Everyone will be wrapped up in talking about them!

Directions:	**Read and follow the instructions on pages 2-8. Print** your request **neatly** on paper and put it in an envelope. You must enclose a **long self-addressed stamped envelope** and **50¢.**
Write to:	The Cherry Tree 9108 Plaza Park Drive Elk Grove, CA 95604
Ask for:	Bellybutton tattoos

Directions:	**Read and follow the instructions on pages 2-8. Print** your request **neatly** on paper and put it in an envelope. You must enclose a **long self-addressed stamped envelope** and **$1.00.**
Write to:	Daisy Enterprises Dept. WT2 P.O. Box 1426 Rutherfordton, NC 28139
Ask for:	Wrist tattoos

School Supplies

Mini Zoo Animals

Can you take an elephant to school? How about a zebra or a lion? You can—if the animals are these cool mini zoo erasers! You'll receive a set that includes four mini erasers shaped like different animals.

Directions:	Read and follow the instructions on pages 2-8. **Print** your request **neatly** on paper and put it in an envelope. You must enclose a **long self-addressed stamped envelope** and **35¢**. *No checks, please.*
Write to:	Lauren & Company Dept. MZE 2 P.O. Box 1019 Mundelein, IL 60060
Ask for:	Mini zoo animal erasers

Aliens

Greetings, earthling! You can use these alien erasers to vaporize your mistakes. And your earthling friends will admire the aliens' out-of-this-world looks! You will receive four alien erasers in different neon colors.

Directions:	Read and follow the instructions on pages 2-8. **Print** your request **neatly** on paper and put it in an envelope. You must enclose a **long self-addressed stamped envelope** and **35¢**.
Write to:	Daisy Enterprises Dept. ALE P.O. Box 1426 Rutherfordton, NC 28139
Ask for:	Alien erasers

ERASERS

Mini Rainbows

Hold a rainbow in your hand with these rainbow-colored mini erasers. You'll receive six erasers shaped like hearts, stars, and rainbows. Use them to erase mistakes or just to collect or trade.

Directions:	Read and follow the instructions on pages 2-8. Print your request neatly on paper and put it in an envelope. You must enclose a long self-addressed stamped envelope and 50¢.
Write to:	Daisy Enterprises Dept. RE2 P.O. Box 1426 Rutherfordton, NC 28139
Ask for:	Mini rainbow erasers

Mini Critters

There's nothing creepy about this offer! Even the most squeamish kid will love to have these mini critter erasers. You'll receive four different erasers of critters like a ladybug, turtle, frog, and butterfly.

Directions:	Read and follow the instructions on pages 2-8. Print your request neatly on paper and put it in an envelope. You must enclose a long self-addressed stamped envelope and 35¢.
Write to:	Daisy Enterprises Dept. CERA P.O. Box 1426 Rutherfordton, NC 28139
Ask for:	Mini critter erasers

Hot Pencil

Heat up your writing by using this awesome heat sensitive pencil. When you touch it, your body heat causes the pencil's designs to change color. This pencil is so cool, it's hot!

Directions:	Read and follow the instructions on pages 2-8. Print your request neatly on paper and put it in an envelope. You must enclose a long self-addressed stamped envelope and $1.00.
Write to:	Daisy Enterprises Dept. THRM P.O. Box 1426 Rutherfordton, NC 28139
Ask for:	Heat-sensitive pencil

State Pencil

You'll have important facts about your state right in your hand with this informative state pencil. You'll receive one pencil featuring your state's capital, bird, flower, and statehood anniversary date.

Directions:	Read and follow the instructions on pages 2-8. Print your request neatly on paper and put it in an envelope. You must enclose a long self-addressed stamped envelope and $1.00.
Write to:	Daisy Enterprises Dept. STATE P.O. Box 1426 Rutherfordton, NC 28139
Ask for:	State pencil (Specify state.)

Question Bookmarks

Why do dogs have wet noses? You'll find the answer to this kind of question on these fun, informative bookmarks. Amaze your friends, family, and teachers when you can answer these puzzling questions. You'll receive five bookmarks.

Directions:	Read and follow the instructions on pages 2-8. **Print** your request **neatly** on paper and put it in an envelope. You must enclose a **long self-addressed stamped envelope** and **$1.00**.
Write to:	Daisy Enterprises Dept. QUBK P.O. Box 1426 Rutherfordton, NC 28139
Ask for:	Question bookmarks

No More Homework! No More Tests!

If you think homework and tests should be banned, wear this button and see if others agree. We can't guarantee the button will wipe out homework and tests, but you'll sure make a statement by wearing it.

Directions:	Read and follow the instructions on pages 2-8. **Print** your request **neatly** on paper and put it in an envelope. You must enclose a **long self-addressed stamped envelope** and **75¢**.
Write to:	Meadowbrook Press 5451 Smetana Drive Minnetonka, MN 55343
Ask for:	*No More Homework! No More Tests!* button

Flicker Ruler

Change the wacky images on this loony flicker ruler with a flick of the wrist. You'll receive one 6-inch flicker ruler that features some of your favorite Looney Tunes characters like Yosemite Sam, Wile E. Coyote, and others.

Stencil Ruler

Need to stop your mind from wandering during geometry class? This 4½-inch stencil ruler will keep you busy drawing stars, circles, triangles, and other shapes. Have fun while you learn about shapes and angles.

Directions:	Read and follow the instructions on pages 2-8. Print your request neatly on paper and put it in an envelope. You must enclose a long self-addressed stamped envelope and $1.00.
Write to:	Daisy Enterprises Dept. LTFR P.O. Box 1426 Rutherfordton, NC 28139
Ask for:	Looney Tunes flicker ruler

Directions:	Read and follow the instructions on pages 2-8. Print your request neatly on paper and put it in an envelope. You must enclose a long self-addressed stamped envelope and 25¢.
Write to:	BNG Rural Route 16, Box 1592E McAllen, TX 78504
Ask for:	Stencil ruler

Name Magnet

If you have a magnetic personality, get your name on this great 3½-by-2-inch laminated magnet. You'll receive one magnet featuring your name and one of these cool border designs: confetti, hearts, music notes, or stars and stripes.

Dinosaur Magnet

Put this realistic-looking dinosaur magnet on your locker or any other metal surface and show your classmates that animals from the Jurassic era (the time when dinosaurs lived) are dino-mite!

Directions:	Read and follow the instructions on pages 2-8. **Print** your request **neatly** on paper and put it in an envelope. You must enclose a **long self-addressed stamped envelope** and **$1.00**.
Write to:	Daisy Enterprises Dept. NM P.O. Box 1426 Rutherfordton, NC 28139
Ask for:	Name magnet (Specify border design **and** print name neatly.)

Directions:	Read and follow the instructions on pages 2-8. **Print** your request **neatly** on paper and put it in an envelope. You must enclose a **long self-addressed stamped envelope** and **50¢**.
Write to:	Daisy Enterprises Dept. DM P.O. Box 1426 Rutherfordton, NC 28139
Ask for:	Dinosaur magnet

Free Rubber Stamps

This offer will have you stamping your feet with joy! You'll receive two free rubber stamps in designs like a snowflake or bluebird. Stamps have easy mounting directions. Use them wherever you want to stamp some fun.

Directions:	Read and follow the instructions on pages 2-8. **Print** your request **neatly** on paper and put it in an envelope. You must enclose a **long self-addressed envelope stamped with 2 first-class stamps.**
Write to:	Ramastamps 7924 Soper Hill Road Everett, WA 98205
Ask for:	2 free rubber stamps

Tiny Rubber Stamps

Leave your mark in different ways with these handy, tiny rubber stamps. You'll receive fifteen stamps, with easy mounting directions, in such fun designs as a paw print, smiley face, and many more. Stomp to the mailbox and order your tiny rubber stamps today!

Directions:	Read and follow the instructions on pages 2-8. **Print** your name, address, and request **neatly** on paper and put it in an envelope. You must enclose **3 first-class stamps (no self-addressed envelope required).**
Write to:	Ramastamps 7924 Soper Hill Road Everett, WA 98205
Ask for:	15 tiny rubber stamps

Reading

Animal Book Clips

Mark your place in *Free Stuff for Kids* or in the other books you're reading with these cute plastic animal book clips. You'll receive three different colorful book clips in wild shapes like a lion, tiger, frog, and many others.

Directions:	Read and follow the instructions on pages 2-8. **Print** your request **neatly** on paper and put it in an envelope. You must enclose a **long self-addressed stamped envelope** and **50¢**.
Write to:	Daisy Enterprises Dept. PAB P.O. Box 1426 Rutherfordton, NC 28139
Ask for:	Plastic animal book clips

Giggle Poetry

Who's the King of Giggle Poetry? Bruce Lansky, that's who! He's created a series of funny poetry book for kids, and you can find out more about these books with this colorful bookmark that features four side-splitting poems.

Directions:	Read and follow the instructions on pages 2-8. **Print** your request **neatly** on paper and put it in an envelope. You must enclose a **long self-addressed stamped envelope**.
Write to:	Meadowbrook Press 5451 Smetana Drive Minnetonka, MN 55343
Ask for:	Funny poetry bookmark

Girls to the Rescue

This exciting series of books bursts with girl power! Each story features a girl who saves the day by solving a problem, getting out of a sticky situation, or even saving a life. This bookmark tells more about the first four thrilling books in the series.

Directions:	**Read and follow the instructions on pages 2-8. Print** your request **neatly** on paper and put it in an envelope. You must enclose a **long self-addressed stamped envelope**.
Write to:	Meadowbrook Press 5451 Smetana Drive Minnetonka, MN 55343
Ask for:	*Girls to the Rescue bookmark*

Newfangled Tales

These fairy tales sure aren't Grimm; they're funny! This collection features stories like the one that tells the real reason why a cranky princess became a Sleeping Beauty. The bookmark tells more about this enchanting series.

Directions:	**Read and follow the instructions on pages 2-8. Print** your request **neatly** on paper and put it in an envelope. You must enclose a **long self-addressed stamped envelope**.
Write to:	Meadowbrook Press 5451 Smetana Drive Minnetonka, MN 55343
Ask for:	*Newfangled Fairy Tales bookmark*

Solar System

Put the whole solar system between the pages of a book. Not only will this bookmark keep your place, but it'll also take you to outer space—when you read the interesting facts about our solar system, that is!

Ocean Animals

Take a dive and learn all about creatures living in the deep blue sea. You'll receive five colorful bookmarks, each featuring a different ocean animal on the front and interesting info about the animal on the back.

Hammerhead Shark   Coral   Killer Whale

Directions:	**Read and follow the instructions on pages 2-8. Print** your request **neatly** on paper and put it in an envelope. You must enclose a **long self-addressed stamped envelope** and **35¢**.
Write to:	Daisy Enterprises Dept. PLAN P.O. Box 1426 Rutherfordton, NC 28139
Ask for:	Planet bookmark

Directions:	**Read and follow the instructions on pages 2-8. Print** your request **neatly** on paper and put it in an envelope. You must enclose a **long self-addressed stamped envelope** and **$1.00**.
Write to:	Daisy Enterprises Dept. OABK P.O. Box 1426 Rutherfordton, NC 28139
Ask for:	Ocean animal bookmarks

Sprocket Man!

Who is Sprocket Man? The superhero who teaches you about bike safety, that's who! Learn everything about being a safe, careful bike rider in this awesome coloring book that's also a comic book with a great story.

Directions:	**Read and follow the instructions on pages 2-8. Print** your name, address, and request **neatly** on a postcard.
Write to:	U.S. Consumer Product Safety Commission Washington, DC 20207
Ask for:	*Sprocket Man* comic book, CPSC341

Money Comics

It doesn't have to cost you lots of cash to learn about money. Read about the history of money and consumer credit with these great comics from the Federal Reserve Bank.

Directions:	**Read and follow the instructions on pages 2-8. Print** your name, address, and request **neatly** on a postcard.
Write to:	Federal Reserve Bank of New York 33 Liberty Street New York, NY 10045
Ask for:	*Once upon a Dime* (if you're in grades 1-6) or *The Story of Consumer Credit* (if you're in grades 7-12).

°ACTIVITY BOOKS

Healthy Lungs

Do you think your lungs can help you breathe easily when they're full of cigarette smoke? Don't hold your breath! Ask for either a No Smoking activity book or a Healthy Lungs poster today and learn to keep your lungs clean.

MADD Coloring Book

Drinking + driving = big trouble! After having alcoholic drinks, a person may not be alert enough to drive safely. But what if that person is supposed to drive you somewhere? Learn how to handle this kind of tough situation in this fun coloring book. It could save your life!

Directions: Read and follow the instructions on pages 2-8. **Print** your name, address, and request **neatly** on a postcard.	**Directions:** Read and follow the instructions on pages 2-8. **Print** your name, address, and request **neatly** on a postcard.
Write to: American Lung Association G.P.O. 596 New York, NY 10116-0596	**Write to:** Mothers Against Drunk Driving 511 E. John Carpenter Freeway #700 Irving, TX 75062
Ask for: Activity book **or** Healthy Lungs poster	**Ask for:** MADD coloring book

INFORMATION

MADD Newsletter

Don't just get mad about the dangers of drinking and driving; get smart with this newsletter from MADD Do puzzles, play fun games, read great stories about celebrities, and much more! Please give your age so you get the right newsletter for you.

Mothers Against Drunk Driving

Directions:	Read and follow the instructions on pages 2-8. **Print** your name, address, and request **neatly** on a postcard.
Write to:	Mothers Against Drunk Driving 511 E. John Carpenter Freeway #700 Irving, TX 75062
Ask for:	M.A.D.D. newsletter (Specify age.)

Drugs Aren't Cool!

You've heard that drugs aren't cool and can mess up your life. Learn more about what drugs do and how to handle peer pressure with these two important, informative pamphlets. Learn the facts and just say no to drugs!

Directions:	Read and follow the **instructions** on pages 2-8. **Print** your request **neatly** on paper and put it in an envelope. You must enclose a **long self-addressed stamped envelope.**
Write to:	Do It Now Foundation P.O. Box 27568 Tempe, AZ 85285-7568
Ask for:	*Are You Drug Smart?* and *All about Peer Pressure & Choices* pamphlets

Disaster Twins!

Look out! Natural disasters happen wherever Julia and Robbie go, and you can read all about their exciting adventures to keep safe. Plus, you'll learn how you can prepare for and stay safe during whatever natural disaster comes your way.

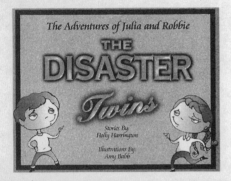

Directions:	Read and follow the instructions on pages 2-8. **Print** your name, address, and request **neatly** on a postcard.
Write to:	FEMA Publications P.O. Box 2012 Jessup, MD 20794
Ask for:	*The Adventures of Julia and Robbie: The Disaster Twins*

More Freebies

Here's what this free catalog from Uncle Sam can give you: over 200 free and low-cost publications on all sorts of topics! Order yours today and see the latest freebies and cheapies the United States government has to offer.

Directions:	Read and follow the instructions on pages 2-8. **Print** your name, address, and request **neatly** on a postcard.
Write to:	The Consumer Information Center The Consumer Information Catalog Pueblo, CO 81009
Ask for:	*Consumer Information Catalog*

Merlyn's Pen

Are you in grades six to twelve and wish your stories, poems, or essays were published in this widely respected magazine? Send for this submissions cover sheet, follow the instructions, and maybe you'll get your wish!

Directions:	Read and follow the instructions on pages 2-8. Print your request neatly on paper and put it in an envelope. You must enclose a long self-addressed stamped envelope.
Write to:	Merlyn's Pen, Inc. P.O. Box 910 East Greenwich, RI 02818
Ask for:	Official Cover Sheet for Submissions

Creative Writing

If you like to get creative with your writing, then this offer's for you. You'll receive guidelines for submitting your writing to *Creative with Words*, a magazine for kid writers. Follow the instructions and maybe you'll see your creative words published!

Directions:	Read and follow the instructions on pages 2-8. Print your request neatly on paper and put it in an envelope. You must enclose a long self-addressed stamped envelope.
Write to:	Creative with Words Publications P.O. Box 223226 Carmel, CA 93722
Ask for:	Creative with Words flyers

Skipping Stones

See the world as writers and artists view it with *Skipping Stones*, a magazine featuring writing, art, and photos from kids around the globe. Order an issue today and start looking at the world in a new way.

Directions:	Read and follow the instructions on **pages 2-8. Print** your name, address, and request **neatly** on paper and put it in an envelope. You must enclose **4 first-class stamps (no self-addressed envelope required)** and **$1.00**
Write to:	Skipping Stones Dept. FSK P.O. Box 3939 Eugene, OR 97403
Ask for:	*Skipping Stones* sample issue

Get Published

Want your talent to be known worldwide? Then submit your writing, artwork, or photos to *Skipping Stones*, an awesome multicultural kids' magazine. With this offer you'll get submissions guidelines and brochure that might help make you famous!

Directions:	Read and follow the instructions on **pages 2-8. Print** your request **neatly** on paper and put it in an envelope. You must enclose a **long self-addressed stamped envelope**.
Write to:	Skipping Stones Dept. FSKG P.O. Box 3939 Eugene, OR 97403
Ask for:	*Skipping Stones* guidelines and brochure

Animals

Saddle Up!

We're not just horsing around with this offer. You'll receive a horse activity book, poster, and bumper sticker if you gallop to your mailbox and order them today!

Tennessee Walker

There's no equal for this equine. (That means horse.) The Tennessee Walking Horse is known for having a gentle nature and being a versatile competitor at horse shows. Learn more about this beautiful animal with this fun activity book.

Directions:	**Read and follow the instructions on pages 2-8. Print** your name, address, and request **neatly** on a postcard.
Write to:	American Quarter Horse Association P.O. Box 200 Amarillo, TX 79136
Ask for:	Horse activity book, poster, and bumper sticker

Directions:	**Read and follow the instructions on pages 2-8. Print** your name, address, and request **neatly** on a postcard.
Write to:	TWHBEA P.O. Box 286 Lewisburg, TN 37091
Ask for:	*Fun with the Tennessee Walking Horse* activity book

DOGS/BIRDS

Kid's Best Friend

Your dog can be a great pal to you, so make sure you'll be a great pal to your dog, too. Get this fun coloring book and checklist bookmark and learn all about preparing your home for your new friend and keeping him healthy and happy.

Directions:	Read and follow the instructions on pages 2-8. Print your name, address, and request neatly on a postcard.
Write to:	American Kennel Club Attn.: Public Education 5580 Centerview Drive Raleigh, NC 27606
Ask for:	*Before You Buy a Dog* coloring book and Responsible Dog Owner's checklist bookmark

Bluebirds

Do you know bluebirds are losing places to nest? But don't be blue! You can help. Learn more about these feathery friends with this great kids' pocket field guide. You'll also get plans to build a nest box. With luck, a bluebird family will move in thanks to you!

Directions:	Read and follow the instructions on pages 2-8. Print your request neatly on paper and put it in an envelope. You must enclose a long self-addressed envelope, stamped with 2 first-class stamps and $1.00.
Write to:	North American Bluebird Society P.O. Box 74 Darlington, WI 53530 also visit www.nabluebirdsociety.org
Ask for:	*NABS Official Pocket Field Guide for Kids* and bluebird nest box plans

Ranger Rick

If you're 7 years old or older and love all kinds of animals, *Ranger Rick* magazine is perfect for you! It's full of fascinating animal facts, games, photos, puzzles, and other fun activities. You'll receive one sample issue.

Directions:	Read and follow the instructions on pages 2-8. **Print** your name, address, and request **neatly** on a postcard.
Write to:	National Wildlife Federation Attn.: Publications 8925 Leesburg Pike Vienna, VA 22184
Ask for:	*Ranger Rick* sample issue

Bite Back!

This 'zine is *grrreat* for kids who want to help make animals' lives better. You'll get one sample issue full of interesting stories about animals and animal rights. Find out what you can do to help animals that can't help themselves.

Directions:	Read and follow the instructions on pages 2-8. **Print** your name, address, and request **neatly** on a postcard.
Write to:	PETA 501 Front Street Norfolk, VA 23510
Ask for:	*GRRR!* sample issue

Elephants

Elephants need your help! They're being hunted for their beautiful ivory tusks and other body parts. Send for this exciting comic about an elephant's life and learn how you can help these big, beautiful beasts stay alive.

KIND News

Learn how you can be kind to nature by ordering this sample newsletter. It features interesting stories about animals, the environment, and even celebrities who are kind to the earth. Kids can make a difference! Please give your age so you get the right newsletter for you.

Directions:	**Read and follow the instructions on pages 2-8. Print** your name, address, and request **neatly** on a postcard.
Write to:	PETA 501 Front Street Norfolk, VA 23510
Ask for:	*An Elephant's Life* comic book

Directions:	**Read and follow the instructions on pages 2-8. Print** your request **neatly** on paper and put it in an envelope. You must enclose a **long self-addressed stamped envelope.**
Write to:	KIND News (FSK) P.O. Box 362 East Haddam, CT 06423
Ask for:	KIND News (Specify age.)

Animal Friend

Pets can be some of the best friends kids have, but are you sure you are a best friend to your pet? You can find out if you get this pamphlet filled with simple tips that ensure your pet's happiness and prevent accidents.

Directions:	Read and follow the instructions on pages 2-8. **Print** your name, address, and request **neatly** on a postcard.
Write to:	PETA 501 Front Street Norfolk, VA 23510
Ask for:	*How Do You Rate As an Animal Friend?* pamphlet

Paw Pals

Become a pen pal with someone who wants to protect animals as much as you do. Get this info on how to start writing to your new friend, plus a pet owner's checklist brochure and an application for free registration in ARK's Animalkind Rescue Kids worldwide humane education program.

Directions:	Read and follow the instructions on pages 2-8. **Print** your request **neatly** on paper and put it in an envelope. You must enclose a **long self-addressed stamped envelope**.
Write to:	ARK-Animalkind Rescue Kids Pen Pal Registration Form P.O. Box 1271 San Luis Obispo, CA 93406
Ask for:	ARK and Animal Pals Pen Pal registration

Don't Dissect; Respect!

Do you believe dissection—cutting up frogs, worms, and other animals—is wrong? Find out about other ways you can learn about an animal's anatomy in this free booklet that includes a cool sticker. Please give your grade so you get the right handbook for you.

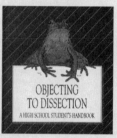

Directions:	Read and follow the instructions on pages 2-8. Print your name, address, and request neatly on a postcard.
Write to:	NAVS-Dissection Hotline 53 W. Jackson Boulevard, #1552 Chicago, IL 60604
Ask for:	*Saying No to Dissection* (if you're in grades K-6) or *Objecting to Dissection* (if you're in grades 7-12)

Rub-Ons

Answer the call of the wild with these fun, full-color animal rub-ons. You'll receive three different rub-ons that can be transferred onto almost any smooth surface, such as a mirror, picture frame, or mug.

Directions:	Read and follow the instructions on pages 2-8. Print your request neatly on paper and put it in an envelope. You must enclose a long self-addressed stamped envelope and 50¢.
Write to:	Daisy Enterprises Dept. RUBO P.O. Box 1426 Rutherford, NC 28139
Ask for:	Animal rub-ons

Wildlife Stickers

Slap these awesome stickers wherever you want to **show your** untamed love for wild animals. You'll **receive** four different wildlife stickers, each displayed on laser-created silver background that makes it sparkle in the light!

Be Kind!

You know you should treat animals kindly. Now let everyone know by sticking these twenty colorful stickers in three different animal designs anywhere you want to remind people animals deserve kindness, too!

Directions:	Read and follow the instructions on pages 2-8. **Print** your request **neatly** on paper and put it in an envelope. You must enclose a **long self-addressed stamped envelope** and **50¢**. *No checks, please.*
Write to:	Lauren & Company Dept. MWAS P.O. Box 1019 Mundelein, IL 60060
Ask for:	Laser wildlife stickers

Directions:	Read and follow the instructions on pages 2-8. **Print** your name, address, and request **neatly** on a postcard.
Write to:	American Humane Association Attn.: Customer Service 63 Inverness Drive East Englewood, CO 80112
Ask for:	Be Kind to Animals sticker sheet

U.S. History and Culture

Stars and Stripes Forever!

Show everyone your patriotic pride by sticking this full-color American flag sticker, which measures 6 by 3½ inches, on folders, car bumpers, windows, or anywhere else you want to display the stars and stripes.

Directions:	Read and follow the instructions on pages 2-8. **Print** your request **neatly** on paper and put it in an envelope. You must enclose a **long self-addressed stamped envelope** and **$1.00**.
Write to:	High Impact Concepts 19332 Harding Lane Huntington Beach, CA 92646
Ask for:	One full-color flag sticker

Country Pride

Are you proud to be an American? Let everyone know with these twenty stickers. All feature a full-color American flag, and some quote, "I'm proud to be an American." Stick them anyplace you want to show your patriotism.

I'M PROUD TO
BE AN AMERICAN

Directions:	Read and follow the instructions on pages 2-8. **Print** your request **neatly** on paper and put it in an envelope. You must enclose a **long self-addressed stamped envelope** and **50¢**.
Write to:	Fax Marketing Dept. 2001 460 Carrollton Drive Frederick, MD 21701
Ask for:	20 American flag stickers

U.S.A.! U.S.A.!

Let's hear it for the red, white, and blue! Show everyone how much you care about the U.S.A. with these six stickers, each featuring patriotic colors and patriotic logos. Slap them on whatever needs a boost of American pride.

Maps

Having trouble remembering where the mainland forty-eight states are located? These stickers can help you put those states in the right places. You'll receive two colorful map stickers of the continental United States, each featuring boundaries and abbreviations.

Directions:	Read and follow the instructions on pages 2-8. **Print** your request **neatly** on paper and put it in an envelope. You must enclose a **long self-addressed stamped envelope** and **50¢**.
Write to:	Daisy Enterprises Dept. USA P.O. Box 1426 Rutherfordton, NC 28139
Ask for:	U.S.A. stickers

Directions:	Read and follow the instructions on pages 2-8. **Print** your request **neatly** on paper and put it in an envelope. You must enclose a **long self-addressed stamped envelope** and **35¢**.
Write to:	Daisy Enterprises Dept. MAPS P.O. Box 1426 Rutherfordton, NC 28139
Ask for:	Map stickers

State Magnet

Whether you live in Maine or Hawaii, Alaska or Florida, or anywhere in between, you can get a colorful magnet that features all kinds of cool information about your state. You'll receive one 2-by-3½-inch laminated magnet.

Directions:	Read and follow the instructions on pages 2-8. Print your request neatly on paper and put it in an envelope. You must enclose a **long self-addressed stamped envelope** and **$1.00**.
Write to:	Daisy Enterprises Dept. STMAG P.O. Box 1426 Rutherfordton, NC 28139
Ask for:	State magnet (Specify state.)

Gettysburg

The Civil War had lots of battles, but the battle at Gettysburg was one of the largest. In this booklet, read what happened during this exciting historic battle and what you'll see when you visit the battleground. You can also read President Abraham Lincoln's Gettysburg Address and General Robert E. Lee's farewell address.

Directions:	Read and follow the instructions on pages 2-8. Print your request neatly on paper and put it in an envelope. You must enclose a **6-by-9-inch self-addressed envelope, stamped with 3 first-class stamps.**
Write to:	Gettysburg CVB Dept. 101 P.O. Box 4117 Gettysburg, PA 17325
Ask for:	Gettysburg booklet

U.S. Park Information

Don't waste your summer parked in front of your TV or computer—get outside and enjoy some of America's awesome national parks. Write to any of the following national parks and receive information that could include maps, brochures, visitors guides, and so on.

Directions: Read and follow the instructions on pages 2-8. Print your name neatly on paper and put it in an envelope. **Write to:** The address is listed below each regional area. **Ask for:** Park guide information.

New England
Acadia National Park
Information Office
P.O. Box 177
Bar Harbor, ME 04609

Midwest
Badlands National Park
Information Office
P.O. Box 6
Interior, SD 57750

Southeast
Biscayne National Park
P.O. Box 1369
Homestead, FL 33090-1369

Rocky Mountains
Canyonlands National Park
2282 South West Resource Boulevard
Moab, UT 84532-8000

Southwest
Big Bend National Park
P.O. Box 129
Big Bend National Park, TX 79834

Discover America

If your family is planning a vacation or if you want to know more about your country, this offer is for you. Write to any address listed here and you'll receive free information about that state. If you ask for school report information, you just might get something extra!

Directions: Read and follow the instructions on pages 2-8. Print your name, address, and request neatly on a postcard. **Write to:** The address listed below each state. **Ask for:** Tourism information and/or school report information.

Alabama
Alabama Bureau of Tourism and
Travel
P.O. Box 4927
Montgomery, AL 36103-4927

Alaska
Alaska Division of Tourism
P.O. Box 110801
Juneau, AK 99811-0801

Arizona
Arizona Office of Tourism
2702 N. 3rd Street, Suite 4015
Phoenix, AZ 85004

Arkansas
Arkansas Dept. of Parks and Tourism
One Capitol Mall
Little Rock, AR 72201

California
Dept. TIA
P.O. Box 1499
Sacramento, CA 95812

Colorado
Colorado Travel and Tourism
Authority
1127 Pennsylvania
Denver, CO 80203

Connecticut
Connecticut Dept. of Economic
Development
Office of Tourism
505 Hudson Street
Hartford, CT 06106

Delaware
Delaware Tourism Office
89 Kings Highway
Dover, DE 19901-0730

Florida
Visit Florida
P.O. Box 1100
Tallahassee, FL 32302-1100

Georgia
Georgia Tourist Division
P.O. Box 1776
Atlanta, GA 30301-1776

Hawaii
Hawaii Visitors and Convention
Bureau
Royal Hawaii Shopping Center
2201 Kalakaua Avenue, Suite A401A
Honolulu, HI 96815

Idaho
Dept. of Commerce, Tourism
Division
P.O. Box 83720
Boise, ID 83720-0093

Illinois
IL Dept. of Commerce and
Community Affairs,
Bureau of Tourism
James R. Thompson Center
100 W. Randolph, Suite 3-400
Chicago, IL 60601

Indiana
Indiana Tourism Division
One N. Capitol, Suite 700
Indianapolis, IN 46204

Iowa
Iowa Dept. of Economic
 Development
Division of Tourism
200 E. Grand Avenue
Des Moines, IA 50309

Kansas
Dept. of Commerce
700 SW Harrison, Suite 1300
Topeka, KS 66603-3712

Kentucky
TRAVEL
Dept. WWW
P.O. Box 2011
Frankfort, KY 40602

Louisiana
Office of Tourism
P.O. Box 94291
Baton Rouge, LA 70804

Maine
L.L.Bean Inc.
Tourism Department
1333 Washington Avenue
Portland, ME 04103-3638

Maryland
Maryland State Office of Tourism
217 E. Redwood Street
9th Floor Skylobby
Baltimore, MD 21202

Massachusetts
Office of Travel and Tourism
State Travel Building
10 Park Plaza, Suite 4510
Boston, MA 02116

Michigan
Travel Michigan
4226 Miller Road, Suite 4
Flint, MI 48507-9821

Minnesota
Minnesota Office of Tourism
121 7th Place East
500 Metrosquare
St. Paul, MN 55101-2146

Mississippi
Dept. of Economic and Community
 Development
Tourism Development
P.O. Box 849
Jackson, MS 39205

Missouri
Missouri Division of Tourism
P.O. Box 1055
Jefferson City, MO 65102

Montana
Dept. of Commerce
Travel Montana
1424 9th Avenue
Helena, MT 59620-0533

Nebraska
Nebraska Tourism Office
P.O. Box 98907
Lincoln, NE 68509-8907

Nevada
Nevada Commission on Tourism
401 N. Carson Street
Carson City, NV 89701

New Hampshire
New Hampshire Division of
 Travel and Tourism
P.O. Box 1856
Concord, NH 03302-1856

New Jersey
New Jersey Commerce and Economic
 Growth Division
P.O. Box 820
Trenton, NJ 08625

New Mexico
New Mexico Dept. of Tourism
P.O. Box 20002
Santa Fe, NM 87501

New York
NYS Division of Tourism
Empire State Plaza
Main Concourse
Albany, NY 12223

SEE THE USA

North Carolina
Division of Tourism, Film, and Sports
  Development
301 N. Wilmington Street
Raleigh, NC 27601

North Dakota
North Dakota Tourism Promotion
Liberty Memorial Building
Capitol Grounds
604 E. Boulevard
Bismarck, ND 58505-0825

Ohio
Ohio Division of Travel and Tourism
P.O. Box 1001
Columbus, OH 43216-1001

Oklahoma
Oklahoma Travel and Tourism
  Division
P.O. Box 60789
Oklahoma City, OK 73146-0789

Oregon
Oregon Tourism Commission
775 Summer Street Northeast
Salem, OR 97301-1282

Pennsylvania
Bureau of Travel Marketing
Forum Building, Room 404
Harrisburg, PA 17120

Rhode Island
Rhode Island Tourism Division
One W. Exchange Street
Providence, RI 02903

South Carolina
South Carolina Dept. of Parks,
  Recreation, and Tourism
1205 Pendleton Street, Suite 106
Columbia, SC 29201

South Dakota
Dept. of Tourism
Capitol Lake Plaza
c/o 500 E. Capitol Avenue
Pierre, SD 57501-5070

Tennessee
Dept. of Tourism
320 6th Avenue N., 5th Floor
Nashville, TN 37243

Texas
Texas Dept. of Economic
  Development
P.O. Box 12728
Austin, TX 78711-2728

Utah
Utah Travel Council
P.O. Box 147420
Salt Lake City, UT 84114-7420

Vermont
Vermont Dept. of Tourism and
  Marketing
6 Baldwin Street
Montpelier, VT 05633

Virginia
Virginia Tourism Corporation
901 E. Byrd Street
Richmond, VA 23219

Washington
Washington State Dept. of Tourism
P.O. Box 42500
Olympia, WA 98504-2500

Washington, D. C.
Washington Convention and Visitors
  Association
1212 New York Avenue Northwest
Washington, DC 20090

West Virginia
Division of Tourism
2101 Washington Street Northeast
Charleston, WV 25305

Wisconsin
Division of Tourism
P.O. Box 7976
Madison, WI 53707-7976

Wyoming
Wyoming Division of Tourism
I-25 at College Drive
Cheyenne, WY 82002

Science and the Internet

Science Weekly

Have fun learning about science with this sample issue of *Science Weekly*, an exciting magazine for kids in preschool through grade eight. Read all sorts of fascinating stories about today's science. Be sure to specify your grade level so you get the right sample issue for you.

Directions:	Read and follow the instructions on **pages 2-8. Print** your request **neatly** on paper and put it in an envelope. You must enclose a **long self-addressed stamped envelope.**
Write to:	Science Weekly, Inc. 2141 Industrial Boulevard, Suite 202 Silver Spring, MD 20904
Ask for:	*Science Weekly* sample issue (Specify grade level.)

Sky Watching

Want to learn more about astronomy or just learn how to identify the Big Dipper? Send for these six book lists and discover some out-of-this-world books about astronomy and space science!

Directions:	Read and follow the instructions on **pages 2-8. Print** your name, address, and request **neatly** on a postcard.
Write to:	Harvard-Smithsonian Center for Astrophysics Attn.: Publications Dept. 60 Garden Street Cambridge, MA 02138
Ask for:	Astronomy and space science book lists

Magnifying Glass

Make small things look bigger with this colorful animal with a magnifying-glass center. Use it to read tiny print like this or to examine stamps or fingerprints more closely. However you use it, this magnifying glass will let you keep an eye on things!

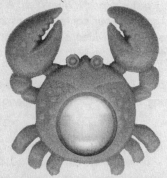

Directions:	Read and follow the instructions on pages 2-8. Print your request neatly on paper and put it in an envelope. You must enclose a long self-addressed stamped envelope and 50¢.
Write to:	Daisy Enterprises Dept. AMG2 P.O. Box 1426 Rutherfordton, NC 28139
Ask for:	Plastic animal magnifying glass

Fossil Embosser

Press into the past with this cool fossil embosser. When you put paper between the halves and press them together, an animal skeleton appears. Press aluminum foil for a really awesome effect!

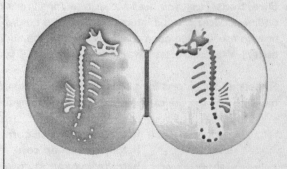

Directions:	Read and follow the instructions on pages 2-8. Print your request neatly on paper and put it in an envelope. You must enclose a long self-addressed stamped envelope and 35¢.
Write to:	Daisy Enterprises Dept. AFS2 P.O. Box 1426 Rutherfordton, NC 28139
Ask for:	Animal fossil embosser

Free Stuff on the Internet

The Internet is the fastest-growing form of communication today—it's also lots of fun. If you have access to a computer that's hooked up to the World Wide Web, you can use the addresses on the following pages to receive lots of fun and interesting stuff for free!

Directions: First, you need access to a computer that's hooked up the World Wide Web. A variety of on-line services provide Internet access. Find out which on-line browser your computer uses and learn how to use it. Then open the browser, type the address into the space provided, and hit **return** (or **enter**). Web addresses always begin with **http://** (and many addresses follow with **www.**).

Sometimes an address for a site will change or completely disappear. If you type in an address and get a message that the site can't be found, try searching for it by starting at one of the following addresses:

Excite	**http://www.excite.com**
Snap	**http://www.snap.com**
Yahoo	**http://www.yahoo.com**
Yahooligans	**http://www.yahooligans.com**
Webcrawler	**http://www.webcrawler.com**

Lots of the sites listed on the following pages require that you fill in your name, address, and e-mail address on an on-line form so you can be sent free stuff by mail. **Before you give any personal information to a site, make sure a grownup sees what information the site wants you to send.** *This is very important!* Even though we've checked out these sites and made sure they're okay for you, it's best if a grownup double-checks them.

Many of the sites listed on these pages allow you to download free software, including video games, screen savers, and other fun stuff. **Again, before you download any software, make sure a grown-up checks it out first.** Here are the types of free downloadable software on the Internet:

THE INTERNET

Shareware: Games and other software that work for a limited amount of time or contain only a portion of the program. Shareware is meant to entice you into buying the whole version of the program (although you don't have to).

Freeware: Full versions of games and other software for free! Sometimes old software is turned into freeware by companies to promote sequels.

Abandonware: Games and other software that are more than two years old and are no longer sold.

Note: The Internet is exciting to explore. It's always growing and changing. But all this activity can mean sites that are here one day could be gone the next. Many sites offer free stuff as a promotion for a limited time. So if you wait a long time and don't get your free stuff by mail that you requested from an Internet offer, you might not ever get it. While this situation is disappointing, you can do something about it. Write a complaint letter to us about a site (see page 7 for directions). The Free Stuff Editors can't let a site know you didn't get your stuff. But we can make sure that we don't include that site in next year's edition.

STUFF BY MAIL

FREEBIES
http://www.gigglepoetry.com
Learn to write funny poetry, then enter your funny poetry in this site's contests. You might win a free autographed book as a prize!

http://www.health.org/gpower/catalog/index.htm
Girls rule! An address book, posters, and stickers are just some of the great Girl Power! items you can receive.

http://www.jellybelly.com/sample_summary.html
Fill out a quick survey and receive a free sample of Jelly Belly jellybeans. Yummy!

http://www.whitehouse.gov/WH/kids/html/write.html
Send a letter to the President, First Lady, or Vice President and you'll receive a response from the White House.

THE INTERNET

http://www.teen.com/special/bookmark.html

This site is the "ultimate place for teens." Send for five free Teen.com bookmarks and you'll be registered to win a free Teen.com T-shirt.

http://www.sportys.com/pilot/free.poster/poster.html

Love planes? Then you'll love getting this free 35-by-23-inch poster of the cockpit of the Cessna 172R, the world's most popular training aircraft.

http://www.b1stgirl.com/form/htm

B*1st makes clothes for girls by girls. Send for a free packet of stickers from this cool company.

http://www.orkin.com/html/idguide.html

Receive an eighteen-page, full-color insect guide that identifies all sorts of creepy, crawly critters.

http://www.mcgruff.org/order.htm

Learn how to stay safe in all kinds of situations with this free McGruff comic book.

http://www.sikids.com

Request a free trial issue of *Sports Illustrated for Kids*, an awesome sports magazine just for kids.

CLUBS

http://www.esticker.com

Get a free pack of cool stickers when you become an eSticker.com member.

http://www.whymilk.com/clubmilk/index.html

Join Club Milk and you'll get a membership certificate, trading cards, and other neat stuff.

http://www.pooks.com/misc/bdaynew.html

Sign up with this birthday club and you'll get a cool gift for your birthday.

http://www.4fishkids.com/fin_club.htm

The Four Fish Fly Free fan club is a great way for kids to learn about music. Join and you'll get a newsletter, stickers, and much more.

THE INTERNET

http://www.stampsonline.com/catalog/stmpr.htm
Sign up for this super stamp collecting club for kids and get a cool 'zine about stamp collecting full of games, facts, and more.

SOFTWARE STUFF

http://www.kidsdomain.com/down/index.html
This site has links to lots of shareware and freeware for arcade games, educational games, and many more games for all ages.

http://www.microsoft.com/kids/freestuff
Here is a site where you can download lots of free fun and educational games plus free software that is required to play many of the games on the Internet.

http://www.familygames.com/free/freegame.html
Download lots of free, fun, nonviolent games from this site.

http://www.familygames.com/share_st.html
This site offers downloads for all sorts of shareware for fun, nonviolent games.

http://www.earthnavigator.com
Have detailed maps of most of the world at your fingertips and visit thousands of web sites anywhere in the world when you download this free interactive program.

http://www.starstonesoftware.com/eots
Chase storms from the safety of your own computer by downloading this free interactive 3D hurricane-tracking program.

http://www.hungryfrog.com/2k/index_frames.htm
You + Hungry Frog Freeware = big fun! Download all sorts of fun games that will help you learn math.

http://dkonline.com/preview/dinohunter/goodies/index.html
Become a Dinosaur Hunter and download images to print, like dinosaur door hangers, labels, and post-cards, for free!

http://www.wolfenet.com/%7epor/foldup.html
Download this free software and create a town. Arrange buildings, make streets and yards, and plan how your town will grow.

http://www.stickerbook.com
Create cool, interactive stories when you download this free software.

http://www.eatsleepmusic.com
If you love to sing, you'll love this site. Download a free karaoke player, two free songs, and twenty song samples.

LINKS TO MORE FREE STUFF

http://www.myfree.com/freekid.html
This site has links to many other free stuff sites and lists all kinds of freebies you can download, request by e-mail, or send away for by mail.

http://www.pointfreebie.com/kids.html
Here is a site where you can find more freebies that you can receive by mail. Definitely worth checking out!

http://www.geocities.com/~tophers-castle/index.html
This site is tons of fun! You can view cool guides for Winnie the Pooh or even Godzilla! It also has links to Star Wars and Pokémon sites as well as links to more free stuff sites.

INDEX

INDEX

More Books Kids Will Love!

Girls to the Rescue, Book #1
Edited by Bruce Lansky

A collection of 10 folk- and fairy tales featuring courageous, clever, and determined girls from around the world. This groundbreaking book updates traditional fairy tales for girls ages 7½–13. **order #2215**

"An enjoyable, much-needed addition to children's literature that portrays female characters in positive, active roles."
—Colleen O'Shaughnessy McKenna, author of *Too Many Murphys*

Newfangled Fairy Tales, Book #1
Edited by Bruce Lansky

This is a collection of 10 delightful fairy tales with new twists on old stories and themes, including a contemporary King Midas who doesn't have time for his son's Little League games, a prince who refuses to marry any of the unpleasant, grumpy, and complaining young women who had slept on mattresses with peas under them, a beautiful princess who is put to sleep for 100 years because she is so cranky, and a clever princess who pays a dragon to lose a fight with a prince so she can marry the man she loves. **order #2500**

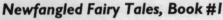

Kids Pick the Funniest Poems

Edited by Bruce Lansky
Illustrated by Stephen Carpenter

Three hundred elementary-school kids will tell you that this book contains the funniest poems for kids—because they picked them! Not surprisingly, they chose many of the funniest poems ever written by favorites like Shel Silverstein, Jack Prelutsky, Bruce Lansky, Jeff Moss, and Judith Viorst (plus poems by lesser-known writers that are just as funny). This book is guaranteed to please children ages 6–12! **order #2410**

A Bad Case of the Giggles

Edited by Bruce Lansky
Illustrated by Stephen Carpenter

Bruce Lansky knows that nothing motivates your children to read more often than a book that makes them laugh. That's why this book will turn your kids into poetry lovers. Every poem in this book had to pass the giggle test with 600 school children. This anthology features poems by Shel Silverstein, Jack Prelutsky, Judith Viorst, and Lansky himself. (ages 6–12)   **order #2411**

No More Homework! No More Tests!

Edited by Bruce Lansky
Illustrated by Stephen Carpenter

This is the funniest collection of poems about school by the most popular children's poets, including Shel Silverstein, Jack Prelutsky, David L. Harrison, Colin McNaughton, Kalli Dakos, Bruce Lansky, and others who know how to find humor in any subject. (ages 6–12) **order #2414**

Look for Meadowbrook Press books where you buy books. You may also order books by using the form printed below.

Order Form

Quantity	Title	Author	Order No.	Unit Cost (U.S. $)	Total
	A Bad Case of the Giggles	Lansky, Bruce	2411	$16.00	
	Free Stuff for Kids, 2001 edition	Free Stuff Editors	2190	$5.00	
	Girls to the Rescue, Book #1	Lansky, Bruce	2215	$3.95	
	Happy Birthday to Me!	Lansky, Bruce	2416	$8.95	
	If Pigs Could Fly	Lansky, Bruce	2431	$15.00	
	Kids' Party Cookbook	Warner, Penny	2435	$12.00	
	Kids' Party Games and Activities	Warner, Penny	6095	$12.00	
	Kids' Pick-A-Party Book	Warner, Penny	6090	$9.00	
	Kids Pick the Funniest Poems	Lansky, Bruce	2410	$16.00	
	Miles of Smiles	Lansky, Bruce	2412	$16.00	
	Newfangled Fairy Tales, Book #1	Lansky, Bruce	2500	$3.95	
	No More Homework! No More Tests!	Lansky, Bruce	2414	$8.00	
	Poetry Party	Lansky, Bruce	2430	$13.00	
	What You Don't About Manners	MacGregor	3201	$6.99	
				Subtotal	
			Shipping and Handling (see below)		
			MN residents add 6.5% sales tax		
				Total	

YES, please send me the books indicated above. Add $2.00 shipping and handling for the first book with a retail price up to $9.99, or $3.00 for the first book with a retail price over $9.99. Add $1.00 shipping and handling for each additional book. All orders must be prepaid. Most orders are shipped within two days by U.S. Mail (7–9 delivery days). Rush shipping is available for an extra charge. Overseas postage will be billed. **Quantity discounts available upon request.**

Send book(s) to:

Name _____ Phone _____

Address _____

City _____ State_____ Zip _____

Payment via:

❏ Check or money order payable to Meadowbrook Press.

❏ Visa (for orders over $10.00 only) ❏ MasterCard (for orders over $10.00 only)

Account # _____ Signature _____ Exp. Date _____

A FREE Meadowbrook Press catalog is available upon request.
You can also phone us for orders of $10.00 or more at 1-800-338-2232.

Mail to: Meadowbrook Press, 5451 Smetana Drive, Minnetonka, Minnesota 55343

Phone 952-930-1100   Toll-Free 800-338-2232   Fax 952-930-1940

For more information (and fun) visit our website: www.meadowbrookpress.com